copyright INFO

Faerie Whispers | poetry for the deep in heart
ISBN 1-59196-129-7
Retail Price $14.95

Published by Instant Publisher, PO Box 985, Collierville TN 38027. Email:questions@instantpublisher.com

Copyright © 2003 by Psychofairy. All rights reserved. No part of this book may be reproduced or transmitted in any form or by any means, electronic or mechanical, including photocopying, recording or by any information storage and retrieval system without written permission from Psychofairy, except for the inclusion of brief quotations in a review. Although every precaution has been taken in the preparation of this book, the publisher and author assume no responsibility for errors or omissions. Nor is any liability assumed for damages resulting from the use of the information contained herein.

Trademark to Psychofairy pending. Any names used in this book are fictitious to protect innocent and any resemblances are purely coincidental. Content in this book are both fiction and non-fiction, depending on material. Almost all content stems from real-life experiences either to Psychofairy or someone she knows/knew. Cover design, all graphic design, layout, photography, poems, words, rantings by Psychofairy. Modeling: Jessi Goodwin. Author's contact information available at: Psychofairy.com

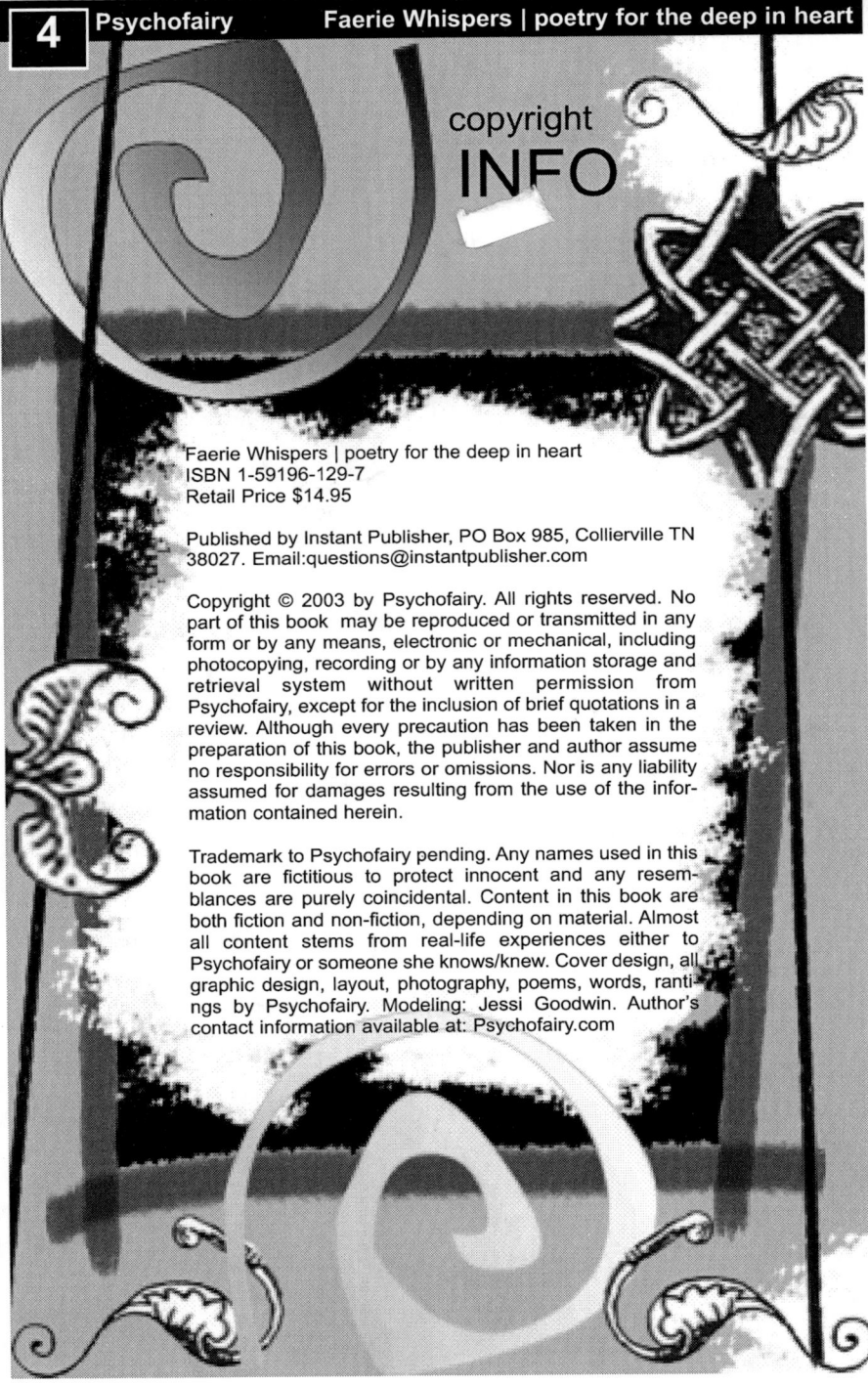

Introduction by Chris Crane

It is my honor to introduce my one true love, Psychofairy to you. She has survived a childhood that could only be described as coming straight from the movie Carrie. With the countless moves of her family and 15 different schools she found herself abused by the ones that were supposed to love her and by her classmates beyond our ability to comprehend. Everything from kids throwing rocks at her for not being able to afford nice clothes to having an abusive mother who forced religion on her and sometimes made her go to church 5 times a week just for "talking back" and countless occasions of verbal and physical abuse. She came from a very broken home and had to live through 3 divorces and watch fathers come and leave from her life.

At the young age of 14, she moved in with her artistic father who nurtured her love for the fine arts. This includes a love for poetry, painting, drawing, wood burning, music, and crafts to mention a few. Together they ran Melting Trees Review (an international poetry magazine) in which she was the associate editor (and then years later she ran it herself). Her love for art developed into a successful career as a graphic artist for major publishing companies including popular magazines, newspapers, and dozens of other publications. These past nine months alone, she has 16 websites to her credit, and several freelance clients as well....All coming from someone who never even went to college. As a poet she has been published over 300 times and as a young teen, she published her first book of poems.

The men in her life put her through a nightmarish hell. She ended up running away 2000 miles from home at 17 to get away from her mother's neglect and constant fights. She got engaged to a man who cheated on her and ripped her apart, then years later, married someone else at the young age of 19 only to find she had entered into a bond with a man she could not love and struggled for years with the sadness and trials of infertility, as well as a constant suffocation of always feeling trapped. Living for years with the torment and anguish of an unhappy marriage and a barren whom her heart has been poured into her passion for creative art and poetry.

Many poems in this book were written while she hid in a closet either at home or as a child -- because as a kid, she feared her mom burning her journals for being "ungodly" and as a married woman, feared her husband would snoop into her private thoughts. I have had the privilege of seeing some of her works never viewed by others and my heart has been moved beyond words. It is my fondest hope that you will treasure this view into the inner most depths of her life as I do. This book is a healing process for her - and is finally learning to discover herself.

I love you, Psycho...love Chris

| 6 | Psychofairy | Faerie Whispers | poetry for the deep in heart |

Follow only

meet the *yourself*

real me ➡

marinate yourself in affection
define yourself in words

Psychofairy | Faerie Whispers | poetry for the deep in heart | 7

Faerie whispers

silver wings, dusted feet, transparent skin

glow when I want to be seen

fly when I need to escape

but at times, want to be different

hide behind this name

create a spirit I want you to know

leave out details people judge

you hear these faerie whispers

and listen for subtle hints

pale flesh, tangled hair, scarred heart

the real me likes invisibility

and I crawl underground

cover myself with soft leaves and grass

unearthing at night, breathing what I've blocked

singing to solemn music, dancing whole-handed

my mood sways like seasons

I crave the scent of mystery,

but for the few who listen, I live to tell

8 | Psychofairy — Faerie Whispers | poetry for the deep in heart

When the Night Whispers

The first time I saw you walk
through the double automatic doors at work,
I felt you walk through me.
You looked better than a fantasy.
Your light, yet brooding eyes held me
and for a second, I could see into a man's soul.
I've known passion and jealousy
so when you showed up in my checkout lane
with an attractive woman
I was sure she was your lover,
resting in your arms every morning.
I wished I could be her, my hair
threading through your dark chest like a tapestry.
I toss in bed alone, wondering if my cheek
will fit your shoulder or if your breath
will be as cool as the ocean.
I've waltzed through your neighborhood
late at night imagining couples lying naked
beneath sheets, talking about children
and I even knocked on your door looking for you -
but an angry housewife thought
I was her husband's mistress
and slammed the door in my face.
Call me crazy, like all my friends do
I'm interested in a much older man.
I fall asleep hoping to hear your voice,
telling me about your day
or asking me to sneak off to a late-night movie
where ushers would leave us alone
during all those love scenes.
I don't understand this
you never call or ask me out
I live on the faint hint of interest
it takes more than roses and movie tickets
to persuade me
I want to be caressed with compliments,
hear your soft request for a kiss,
but the days pass, not the disappointment.

Psychofairy   Faerie Whispers | poetry for the deep in heart   9

Hubby

my husband spills my drink with his foot
and apologizes before I can react
he knows how I get when he messes up
my computer received a virus today
took a couple Xanax pills so I wouldn't
walk around like a prude.
I've got a temper so strong
it could lift this town and carry it to China,
some people say I get my temper from my mom
others think I've just got issues
yeah, I do have issues! You would too if
every time you come home, the house
looked like it was in the middle of remodeling,
and every time you wake up, you're ten minutes
behind schedule, and every time you go to work
the same coworker calls you a kid even though
you know you're smarter than the old dirtbag.
You'd have issues too if the laundry never got done
and you have to scramble around the house to find
a matching skirt, hell -- you'd have issues too if
you knew you couldn't have children, but the rest
of the world can, including your sworn enemy
who flaunts it in your face! I know this can't just
be me in this bubble of life,
surely someone else has issues too!

10 | Psychofairy
Faerie Whispers | poetry for the deep in heart

Breathe

to breathe, to whisper
to know only one
can exist,
two play this game
share vows that fade
behind an enviable marriage
the rings,
the father, the pillow
all that flickered will
continue to glow
forever will
become invincible

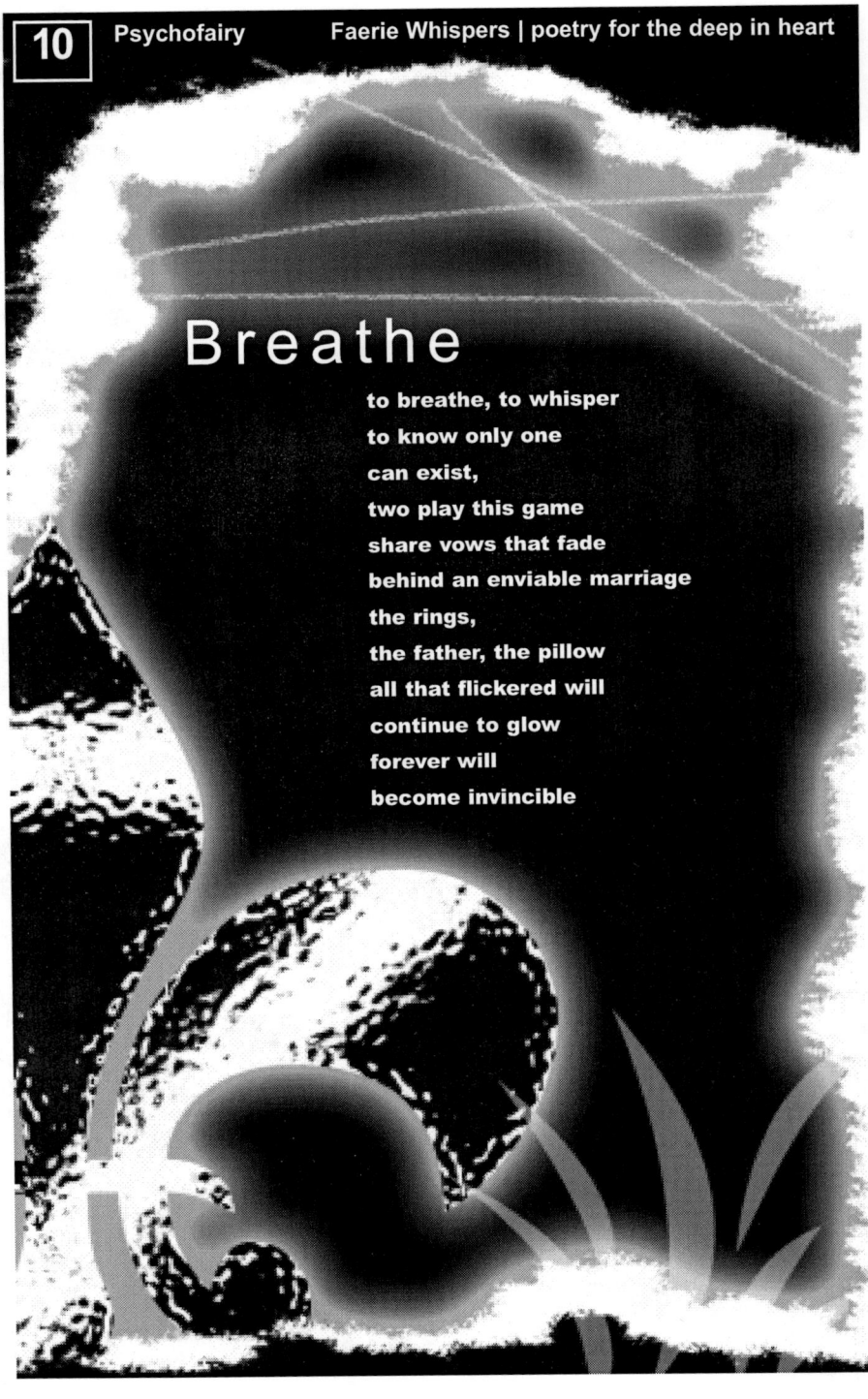

Psychofairy Faerie Whispers | poetry for the deep in heart

Death in San Jose

I will die in San Jose
a city with much pollution
on a Saturday night after a blind date.
It will be a week or two after college starts
and my friends and I in the co-ed dorm
will be held at gunpoint
by a group of drunk maniacs.
They'll brainwash me like Patty Hurst
and make me rob local banks
then I will get caught
and strapped to the
electric chair
but it won't kill me.
They they will try the gas chamber
but I still live.
So instead of releasing me to the streets
where people will see me as a freak,
they will inject poison into my arm
with a sharp, sterile needle,
and I will throw my head back,
jolting and shaking
with white foam seeping from my mouth
and whisper....
I'm innocent.

Psychofairy — Faerie Whispers | poetry for the deep in heart

Calling All Angels

you have become my sanity,
my trophy, my Emmy award
even the angels want us together
and they clear the cracks
in the tundra beneath our steps
to let us walk barefoot on damp ground

I would deny breath
if I could sculpt just ten seconds of eternity
your sweetness murmurs like churchbells
I wait eagerly to be rung
to create music
humming harmonious sounds

I could never miss this earth
knowing love like this
could forever be bronzed...
this love is beyond organic
you are the shape of my fingernails
and I am the olive in your hands

it's too late tonight
beneath these subtle reflections
to walk blindly toward the moon
let's stroll like silk
paving a trail through these trees
professing words we truly mean

Psychofairy | Faerie Whispers | poetry for the deep in heart | 13

Impressions

Imagine what he's thinking

over there serving martinis

to those aged femmes.

He knows they've been sitting

there since his shift started

and his tip jug is almost full...

all the drunk men who had

scooted their stools beside

them for a little flesh-to-flesh

are gone, rejected with the toss of hair.

The women aren't pretty

in fact, he wasn't sure they WERE

women at first,

but he knows what's going on

as he chunks the girl's glasses

with final olives...

those men came and left

with nothing, but the

not-so-elegant ladies

left with the only

compliments they've

had all week.

14 | Psychofairy
Faerie Whispers | poetry for the deep in heart

Frequently

Frequently, like bricks
we sit quietly and silent
holding ourselves
hugging our heads
filtering the mortar
with thoughts

Often, like drops
run swiftly on glass,
pouring ourselves
down drains
emptying our lives
into large tanks

Always, like doorknobs,
we open and close
but never turn -
just fix ourselves
frustrated by nuts and bolts
that allow others to enter
but never us

Psychofairy | Faerie Whispers | poetry for the deep in heart | 15

The Trail of Your Footsteps

Your footsteps
graved in the ground
become peaceful angels
following the blonde star's glint
as your shadow becomes
a silhouette -
a four-month-dead betrayal
to the sun

Your spicy cologne
still moves
like a bouquet of violet
dancers...
melting like ice on pine,
trickling drops of salt
as they kiss the Earth
with your rosemary lips

Your melodic acid still races
between hairs on your
arms
to corduroy -
snug against your thighs.

Eyes of burgandy
tears of rust
my parallel fists
forgive my blindness
as your footprints
fill with dew.

Psychofairy — Faerie Whispers | poetry for the deep in heart

Eden

Daffodils perfume the air

with their sweet aroma

tiptoeing to Eve

and her hubby.

Their naked bodies are smooth

like streams at dusk.

Eve is humming a hymn

while the harmonious bird chirp along

providing music that

echoes off trees.

Brooks trickle through rocks,

beneath bramble bushes

as they carve their own canals

preparing for the belle.

Her toes are dancing over grass

as she throws a grape

and catches it in her mouth.

Adam's across the field

learning to juggle coconuts

while squirrels beneath him wait

for one to fall and break

so they can feast.

Cold rain begins to shower

and the two twirl like children --

spinning as if they were born yesterday.

Psychofairy — Faerie Whispers | poetry for the deep in heart

eve

It has been a while since
the sun kissed
me
and palm trees
dripped dew

Most mornings
clouds wrap in water
as if cotton balls
doused

Adam's surfboard floats
out to sea
mint green and lemon yellow
carry him closer to the horizon

I can see his tan lines
from the shore
where my unpainted toenails sink
into white sand and dark sea foam

His bronzed back bows and
ivory cheeks clink --
too colorful too comment

I lie here, in love,
my stomach sketched in sand
I want to taste the sun
savor the moon, swallow
the coconut's soft, white flesh

The earth splits into halves
with the fruit
Adam, poised on the board,
falls
and I swear in a new language

Psychofairy — Faerie Whispers | poetry for the deep in heart

Austin, My Hero
(for Sami Brady of Days of Our Lives)

Carrie, my sister the saint -
to the world and to her mirror
but she will never be righteous
in my eyes...or Will's.
She sees Austin as the moon,
as I see him as my right
my reward for deception
my prize for schemes.
Austin cradles "our" baby,
but only Carrie holds his heart -
they think I'm cold, ruthless
insensitive to their feelings
uncaring to their wants
selfish to my whims
but it's Austin who leaves me lonely
and Carrie who makes me cruel.
There are days I just want to cry
cuddle my knees to my chest
sit on the bathroom floor
and sulk for hours until Austin
comes, longing for me...
maybe one day he'll realize
how much I want him
and perhaps some day he'll see
how much he loves me.
I will be his fantasy
no longer his nightmare
or bad luck that never ends
I will be the woman in his dreams
galloping on a jeweled horse
with him seated behind me
arms befriending my waist
but right now he sees only Carrie
in a garlic-scented kitchen
cooking a meal and lighting candles
She expects him home tonight
so their love can be rekindled,
but my flame grows stronger
while hers slowly dies -
this will be the evening
all my plans work
this will be the night
that lasts till dawn
and all my prayers will be answered
and I will become Austin's queen,
his hero, his blessing, his love.

Life

been saved

by God so many times

even though once was enough

partly because I'm terrified

of flames and heat

of sorrow and hate

of eternity and regret

now the fear follows

and I don't understand

the whole meaning

but no one will listen

except the silence

of my car as I drive home.

I pray aloud

hoping He hears me

that if I were to crash

on my way there

He's peek through the

glass hole of His mighty door

and invite me in

Psychofairy | Faerie Whispers | poetry for the deep in heart

COWS

The country is no place
for a city girl with growing needs for
excitement and common sense.
She needs a condo in a
30-story building that
overlooks policemen arresting drunks
and overpriced drag queens
trying to get little sausages
in full moons before sunrise.
She needs to carry a stun gun
to protect herself from night-trotters
and a spray of mace as back-up.
She needs to hear women nagging,
men whining, phones ringing,
babies crying, cabs honking,
drivers hollering, bosses threatening,
saxophonists playing, and young
waitresses popping gum...
But no.
She's in the country now
with cows mooing across the street
because her in-laws like sirloin
but if she were to stand outside tonight
she would hear nothing.
I bet she's never heard that.

Psychofairy — Faerie Whispers | poetry for the deep in heart — 21

Raspberries in Waiting

I love him the way
sweetness does a ripe raspberry,
right after a redeeming sunrise.
I am the refined juice inside,
softly poised in the berry's harbor
saturated in soft, floating syrup.
He is the riveting red outside,
the tangible, committed color
that mimics morality.
He dawdles through untainted love.
I wriggle in it.

Predictions

We smoke our cigarettes
and talk about psychics
a thirty-minute phone call
filled with skepticism and truth
the slim line
between puppy shit and poverty
to predict three pregnancies and
unexpected financial gain
in December or January
that our health is fine
our spouses discontent
and we dwell on the past.
They ask more questions
than they answer,
leave hope of children
and new money
keep eyes fixed on the only
dream we can't afford --
so we puff our cigarettes
beside telephones
that will tell us
exactly what we want to hear.

Psychofairy   **Faerie Whispers | poetry for the deep in heart**

The host takes another sip of brandy,
twirls in his swivel chair,
raises his shot glass to the mirror -
cheers -
and swallows the heap
as though it were his last.
The dragging cigar in his mouth
has evolved into an over-aged pacifier
his guests chomp on shrimp cocktails
and egg rolls served on platinum trays
but none is offered to me.
Ladies waltz in candlelight,
giving their flesh a rosy glow
and glistens off their lips as they
rat on about alimony payment
and designer perfumes...
my pearl choker is no competition
for their laced boots, burgundy
dresses, and ruby hair-pieces.
My date staggers to another woman,
adjusting his vodka-stained trousers
and paisley waistcoat
and I hide behind velvet drapes
   with the moon on my back
      and a steel blade in my hands
         waiting for someone to
           make a wrong move.

The Tenth Commandment

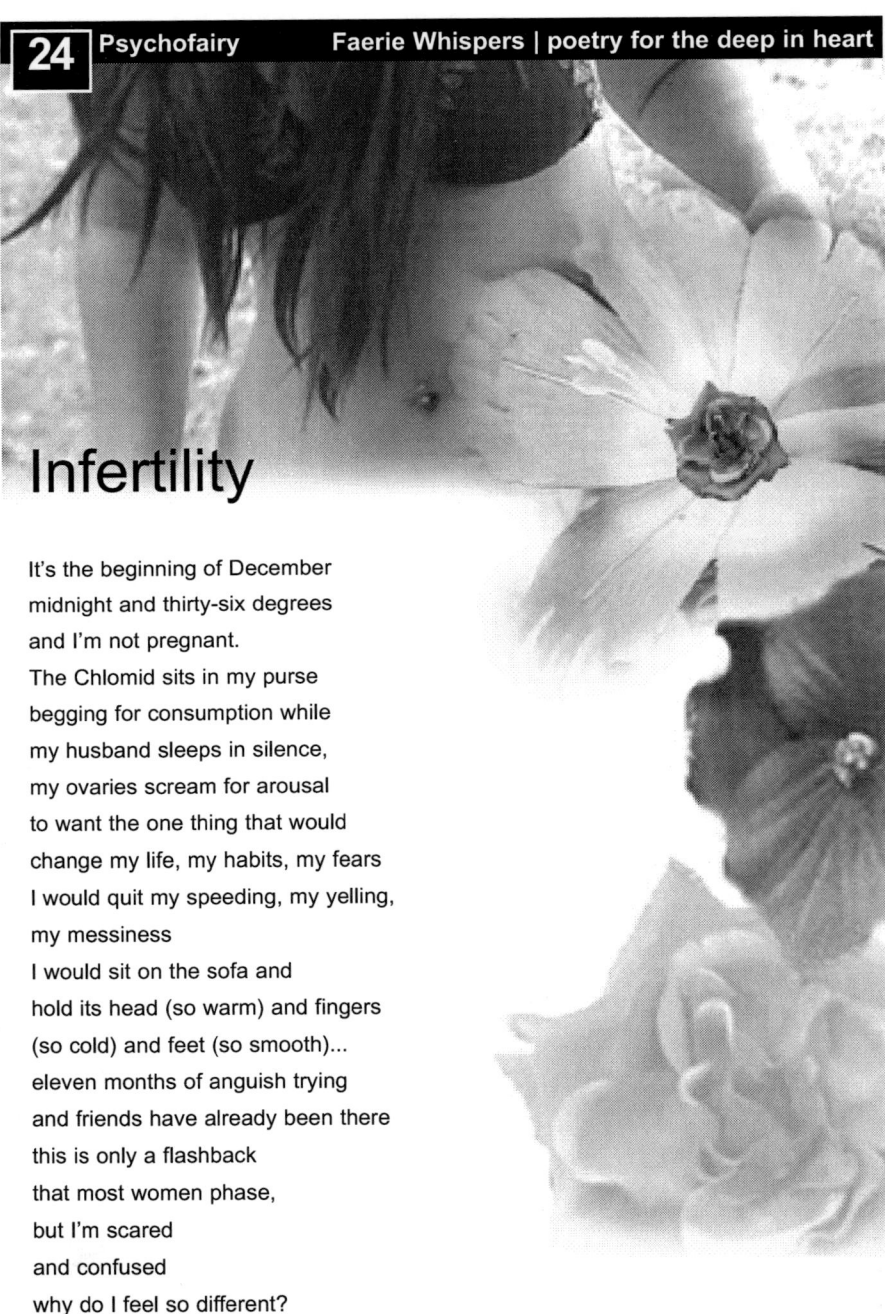

Infertility

It's the beginning of December
midnight and thirty-six degrees
and I'm not pregnant.
The Chlomid sits in my purse
begging for consumption while
my husband sleeps in silence,
my ovaries scream for arousal
to want the one thing that would
change my life, my habits, my fears
I would quit my speeding, my yelling,
my messiness
I would sit on the sofa and
hold its head (so warm) and fingers
(so cold) and feet (so smooth)...
eleven months of anguish trying
and friends have already been there
this is only a flashback
that most women phase,
but I'm scared
and confused
why do I feel so different?
has God made me special?
Lord, please fix me

Loyalty

Last year's spirit climbs stairs in her mind,

hoping to release the past --

unlocking hinges of a steel gate that

blocked her memory like a boulder.

Breathing quietly, trying not to disturb

conversations initiated by her lost love,

she listens for hidden meanings,

hoping to discover an engram never heeded

like old garments spotted at second glance.

The aroma of crushed velvet draws her close

as she tastes the air, clean as satin,

whispering personal praises,

igniting a flame never doused

with uncertainty.

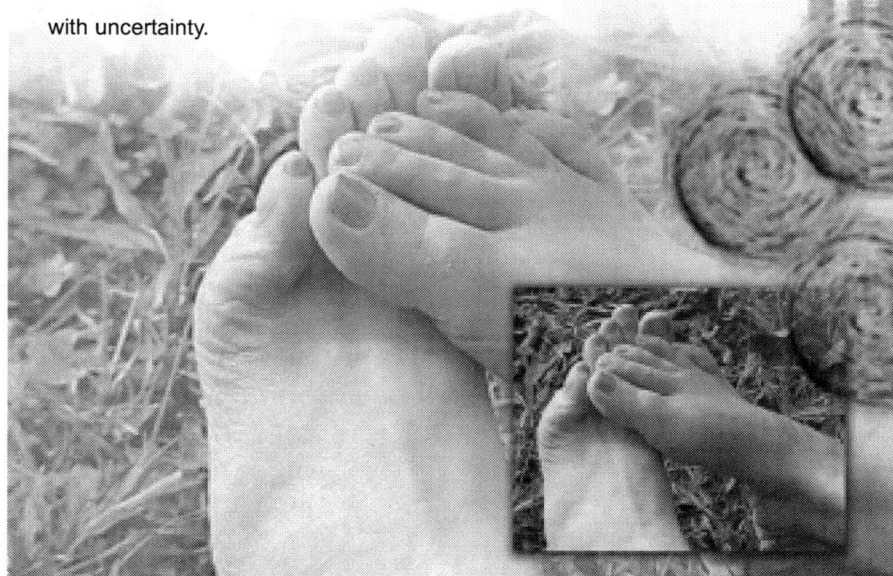

Our Minds on Paper

We stroll in with
loose laser paper
and fading ball-point pens
to chairs in the
conference room.
Ten of us huddled around
our supervisor like children
expecting daddy's wallet.
He talks and we write.
I sketch a house
with trim and doors.
Down the table,
one place setting
of paper to another,
doodles of superheroes
and celebs.
Every week we do this.
Rendering with pencils,
drawing with pens -
tracing our imagination.
He'll discuss our bonuses
and overtime -
yet we continue to ink,
focusing our eyes to the
low level of paper,
trying to act modest
to sounds of monetary praises.
Then we leave our meeting
and toss our sketches away -
for the bucket to
read our imagination.

Special

I imagine you perfect
invincible to anger, fights
and harsh words ranted
always sweet and cherished
everyone crowding to hold you
grandparents choking up as they
touch your head, fingers
and decide whose eyes you have
but I would hold you closer
brush your hair gentler
hum songs softer
read stories longer
and rock you quieter
knowing you are a miracle -
not from medicine
but from God,
no more specialists, no more pills
He has given His prescription

Psychofairy | Faerie Whispers | poetry for the deep in heart

Hard

I felt you between sheets
like discovering the barbed wire
between wooden fence posts,
shocking sharp and precise...
your body has become soft
like mushy, damp ground
yet a part of you stays
so intact, so firm, so ripe
I feel you below handmade pillows
below the comfort of cotton
below the richness of security,
I reach out to boldly caress
the one thing that makes you oblivious
the one thing that forgives your mistakes
the one thing that is supervised by your mind
and it trembles, nervous and anxious
as it waits impatiently for the touch

Sensitive Lands

Leaves frozen in snow

crucial to the ground's color -

sunrises glide over oceans,

gleaming reflections

to France and beyond.

I could be blind

and still see streams

of nature's carved strangers,

knotted trees

turn in spirals

the lingering leaf

refuses to fall

gaudy grass

that stands alone

dark clouds

anguished sun

murky forest walls --

I could find peace

within these pines

if I were blind.

30 | Psychofairy   Faerie Whispers | poetry for the deep in heart

Perfect Spot

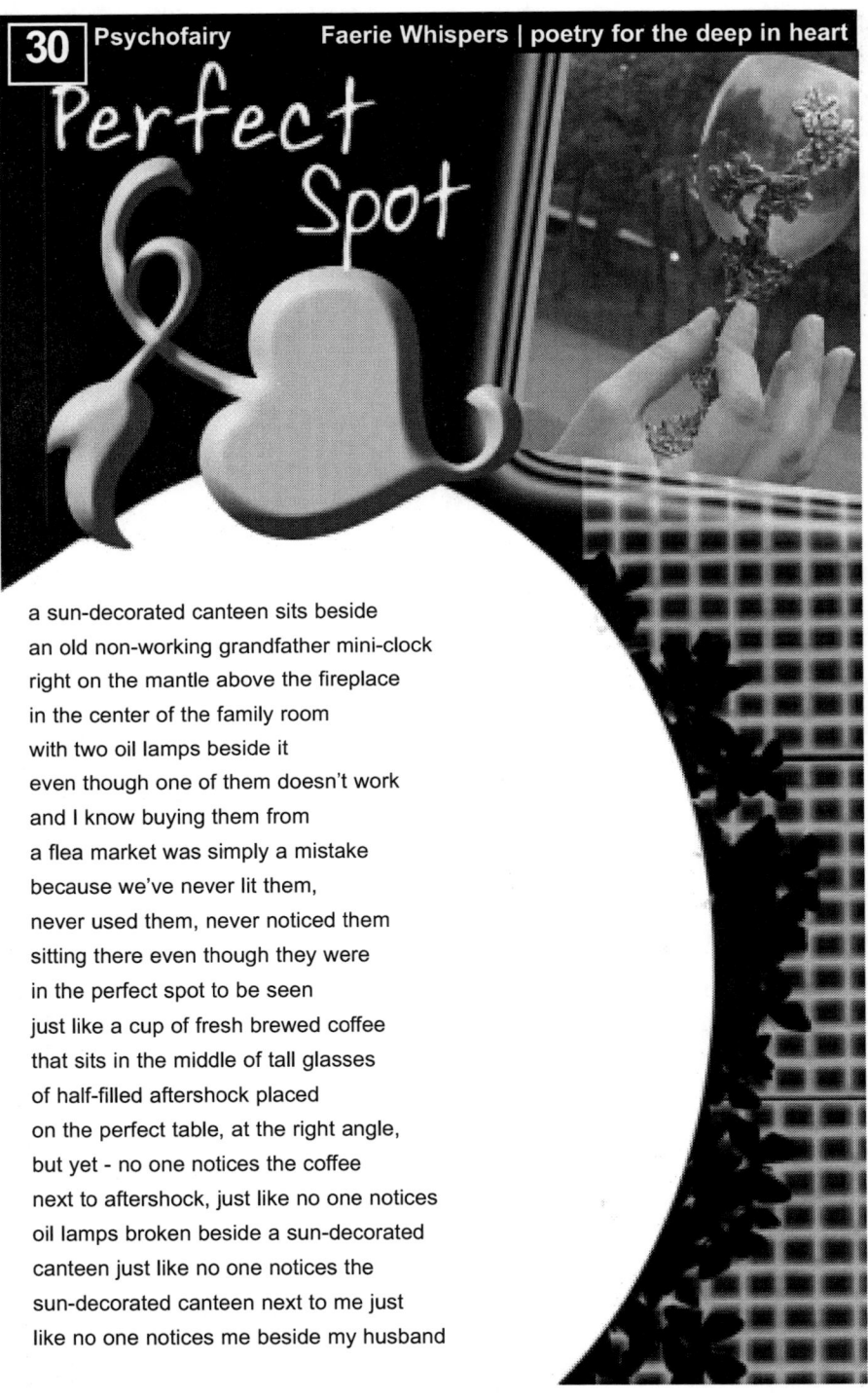

a sun-decorated canteen sits beside
an old non-working grandfather mini-clock
right on the mantle above the fireplace
in the center of the family room
with two oil lamps beside it
even though one of them doesn't work
and I know buying them from
a flea market was simply a mistake
because we've never lit them,
never used them, never noticed them
sitting there even though they were
in the perfect spot to be seen
just like a cup of fresh brewed coffee
that sits in the middle of tall glasses
of half-filled aftershock placed
on the perfect table, at the right angle,
but yet - no one notices the coffee
next to aftershock, just like no one notices
oil lamps broken beside a sun-decorated
canteen just like no one notices the
sun-decorated canteen next to me just
like no one notices me beside my husband

Psychofairy   Faerie Whispers | poetry for the deep in heart   **31**

again

More blood work, more ultrasounds

the stirrups have become my friends

more drugs, more prescriptions

the pharmacy knows me by name

have sex tomorrow night, they say

then it will happen

32 Psychofairy — Faerie Whispers | poetry for the deep in heart

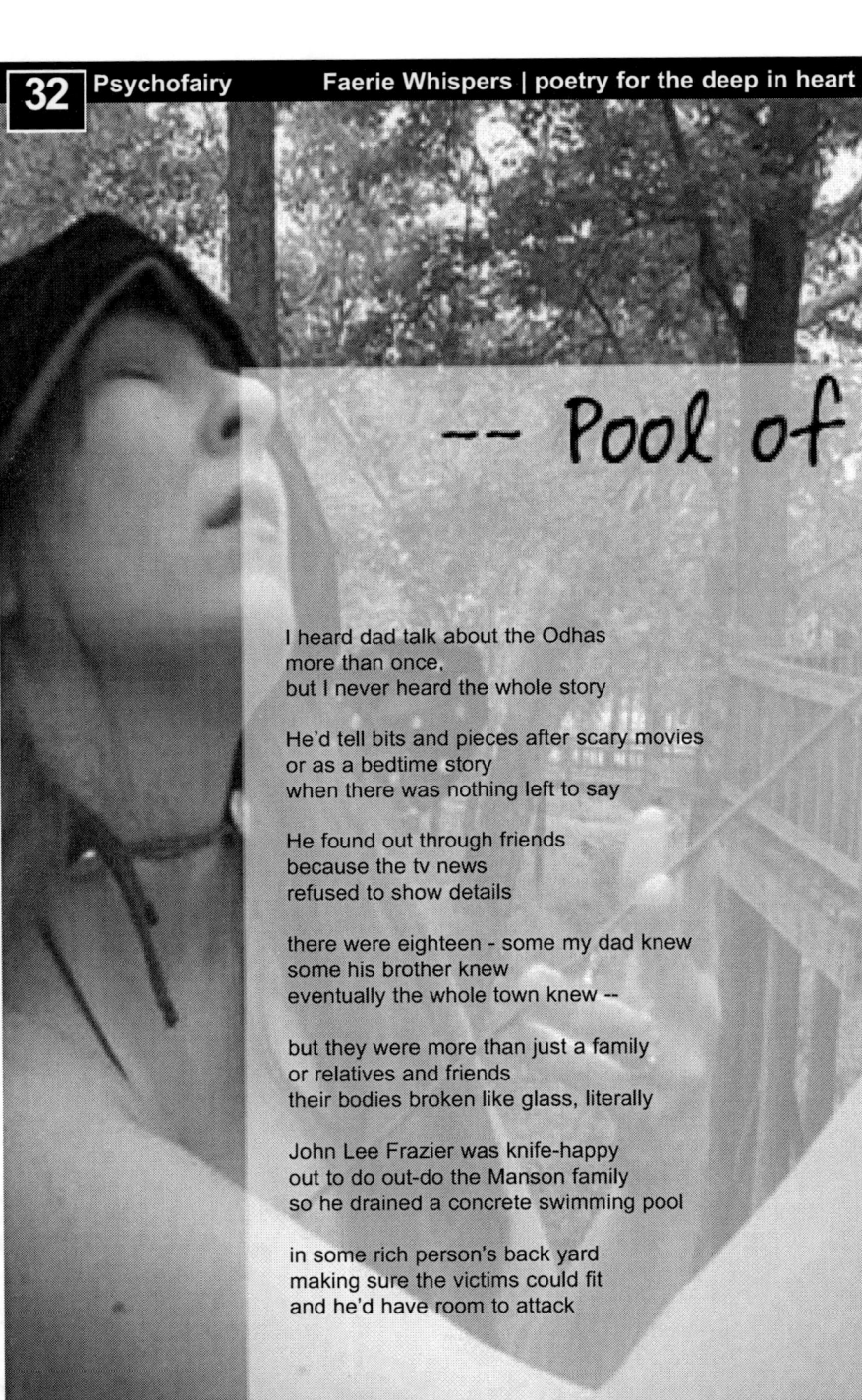

-- Pool of

I heard dad talk about the Odhas
more than once,
but I never heard the whole story

He'd tell bits and pieces after scary movies
or as a bedtime story
when there was nothing left to say

He found out through friends
because the tv news
refused to show details

there were eighteen - some my dad knew
some his brother knew
eventually the whole town knew --

but they were more than just a family
or relatives and friends
their bodies broken like glass, literally

John Lee Frazier was knife-happy
out to do out-do the Manson family
so he drained a concrete swimming pool

in some rich person's back yard
making sure the victims could fit
and he'd have room to attack

| Psychofairy | Faerie Whispers | poetry for the deep in heart | 33 |

Blood --

how did one man
force eighteen people into a pool
with a knife?

he killed the oldest first
to make the children scream -
he always enjoyed the sound of fear

he stabbed each person
and let their blood
slowly feel the pool

that's when I told dad to stop
I didn't want the same nightmares
he still has -

especially since Frazier's
up for parole this fall
with two other mass murderers

no one talks about what happened
I guess it was too awkward
but the town still waits

for the blindfolds of justice to finally be removed
when Frazier sees electric sparks
or is injected with a poisonous needle

34 | Psychofairy   Faerie Whispers | poetry for the deep in heart

frustration
there's no other way around it
morning clocks
afternoon rush
nightly rituals
same showers
same conversations

tuesdays
are like thursdays
only longer
and money
doesn't care
what day it is
only that it needs
to be spent

music
a cross between
poetry and motion
can be played

at any given time
on any given day
and if its words
are heard
REALLY heard
then the day
will change

lyric
that one line
completely changes
the mood
the setting
the rituals
because one line
defines a life
and the intensity
in its release
gives a deeper meaning
to a true
listener

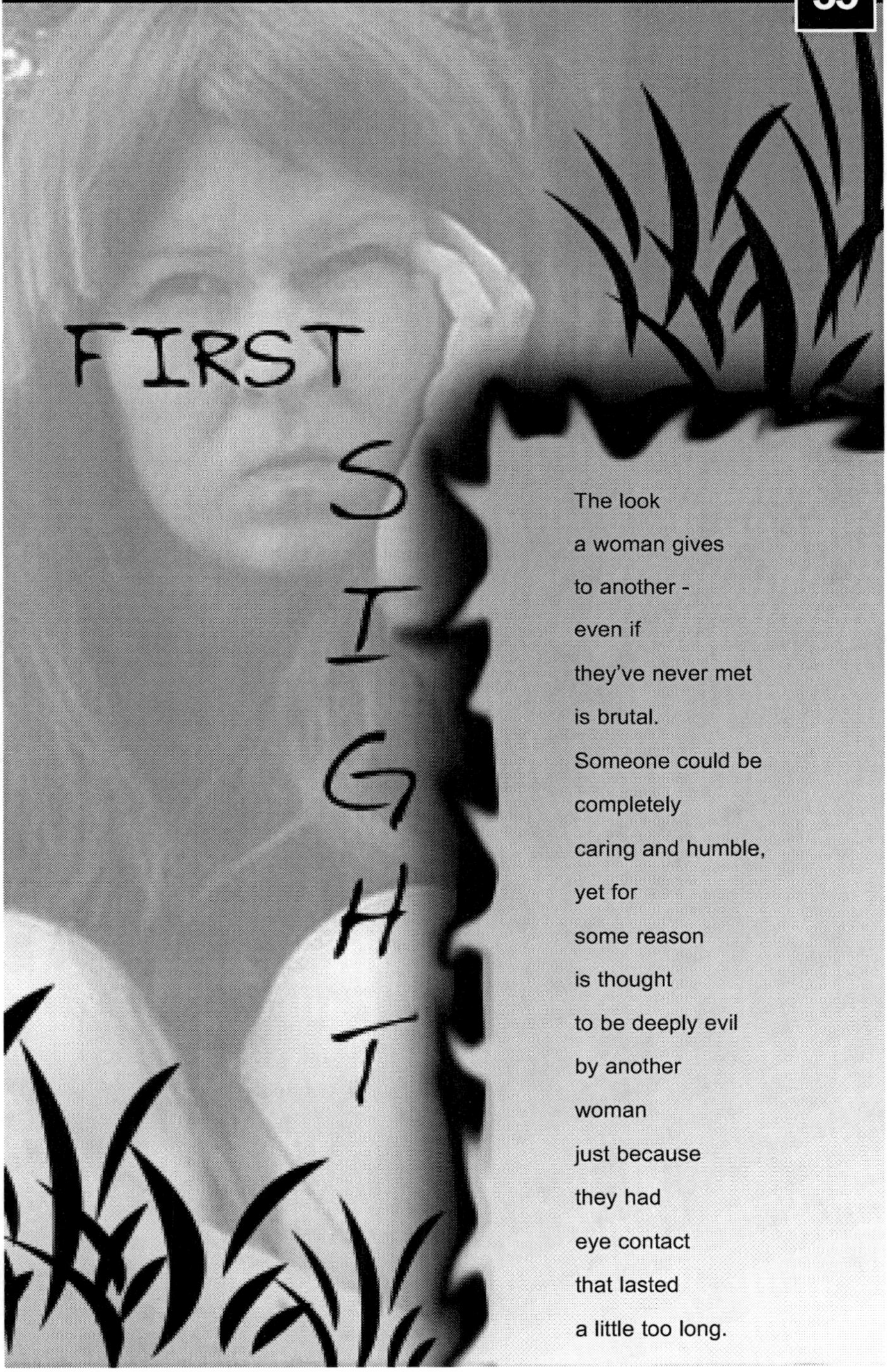

Psychofairy — **Faerie Whispers | poetry for the deep in heart** 35

FIRST SIGHT

The look
a woman gives
to another -
even if
they've never met
is brutal.
Someone could be
completely
caring and humble,
yet for
some reason
is thought
to be deeply evil
by another
woman
just because
they had
eye contact
that lasted
a little too long.

Psychofairy   Faerie Whispers | poetry for the deep in heart

Evelyn

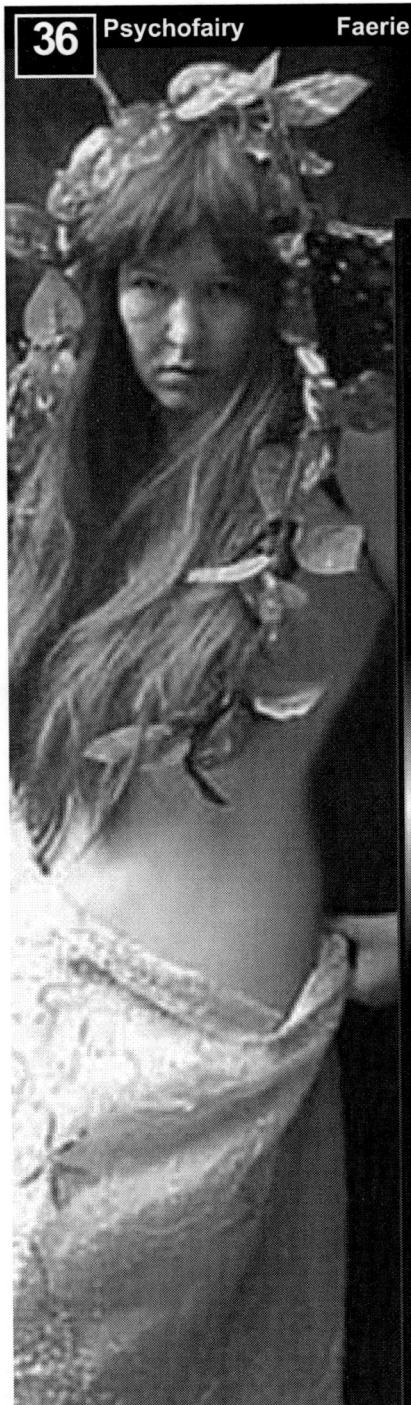

She has botanical beauty

made from fine

oils and perfumes,

perfected with lotions,

cleansed with creams.

Nails filed short

with a clear, plastic shine -

diamonds glisten

from her ears

like small treasures

she looks oriental,

perhaps a ceramic vase

styled and painted

with light colors

boldly proclaiming

they're pastel and proud.

she looks calm,

too satisfied to smile

in her white dress -

long and flowing

dancing around her ankles

completed with sandals that

kiss her toes -

content with life.

Man Crossing the Street

Moving slowly over speed bumps,
my Saturn wheels to a stop,
I let a group of wanderers -
businessmen, teens and mothers
cross in front of me
to do their weekly browsing
but there was one fellow,
an older man who paused,
knelt on the ground,
picked up a dirty milk carton
and frayed grocery bag
flattened by feet and tires...
I sat there amazed that one man
out of a crew of strangers
respects his surroundings
so much, he stopped in front
of a crowd of cars and people
to throw away what we've
so thoughtlessly disregarded,
then continue with his shopping
without a simple thank you.

38 Psychofairy   Faerie Whispers | poetry for the deep in heart

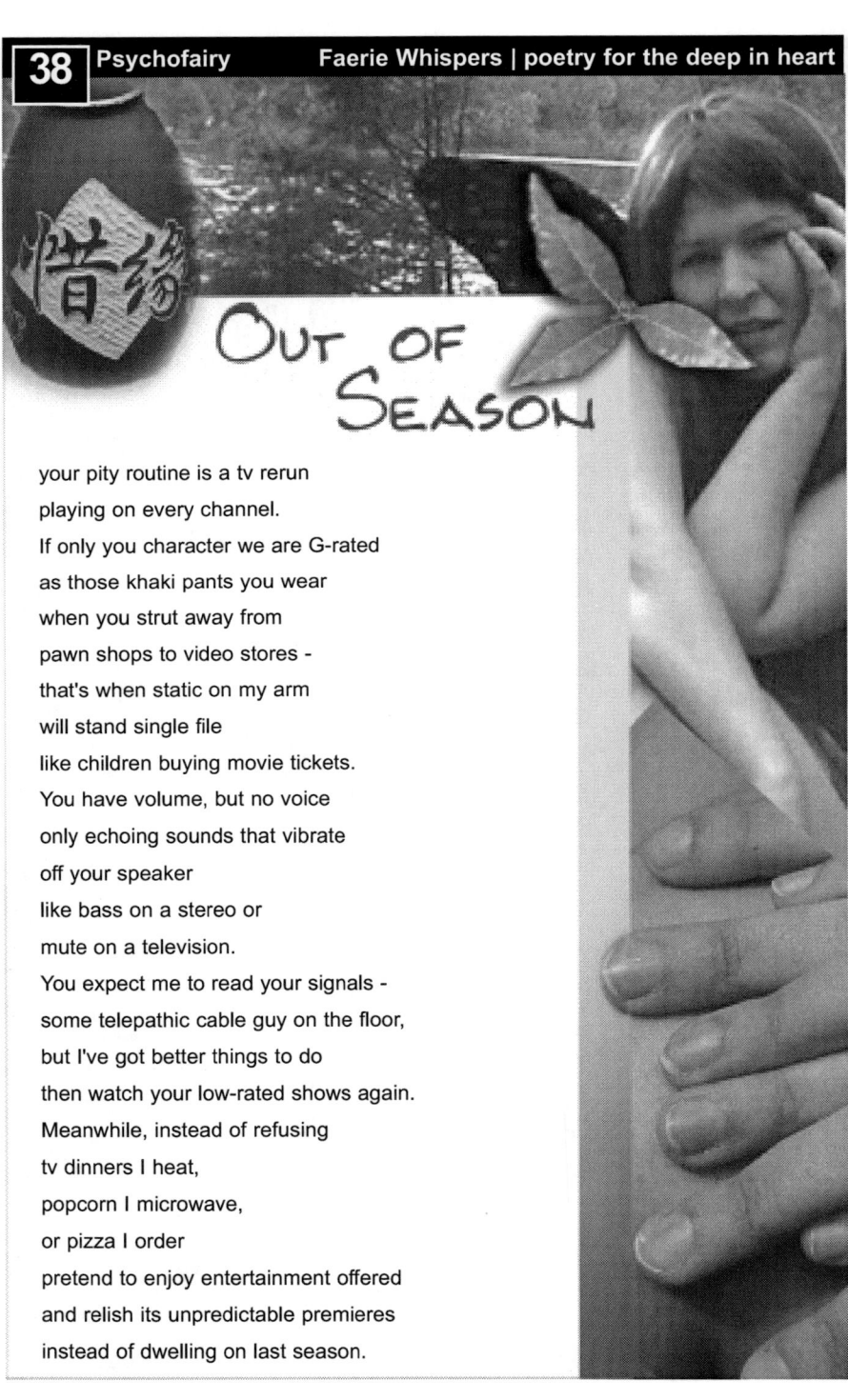

Out of Season

your pity routine is a tv rerun
playing on every channel.
If only you character we are G-rated
as those khaki pants you wear
when you strut away from
pawn shops to video stores -
that's when static on my arm
will stand single file
like children buying movie tickets.
You have volume, but no voice
only echoing sounds that vibrate
off your speaker
like bass on a stereo or
mute on a television.
You expect me to read your signals -
some telepathic cable guy on the floor,
but I've got better things to do
then watch your low-rated shows again.
Meanwhile, instead of refusing
tv dinners I heat,
popcorn I microwave,
or pizza I order
pretend to enjoy entertainment offered
and relish its unpredictable premieres
instead of dwelling on last season.

Forgotten Love

When you said she hurt you
I imagined your heart
walking over broken pine needles
while each wooden needle punctured
it with jagged cuts.

When you convinced me you
had no feelings for her,
I pictured a woman lacking beauty
with bulging stretchmarks
and thinning hair.

You spoke of her in the past tense
like your feelings were washed away
by the salty waves of the ocean
and even mermaids couldn't mind them.

You hugged me, then turned away
like you discovered an imperfection.
I then realized
I was your lost and forgotten love
and it was time to let go.

Psychofairy — Faerie Whispers | poetry for the deep in heart

The Code of Silence

Mike Catalano, a world-renowned poet - and I wrote this poem together while waiting for our food at Applebees. We wrote on a napkin. Some lines are his, some are mine. There is an asterisk* by every line that is his)

He stares at her, wondering if she sees him;
she stares back, wondering why the rudeness.*
The menu becomes his companion
as he pretends to be interested in it.
She looks past the window, without pretense*
like something more important is happening outside.
Although her shadowed image
lies in the corners of his tired eyes,
he still isn't satisfied.
She sees his examination, as if*
she were a goldfish in a private aquarium.*
They pick up their frosted mugs
full of stale root beer and sip slowly
while she wishes he would pick up the check*
and that she could shut him, once and for all,*
forever from her life.*
And he wishes she'd walk into his -
but he knows only a muscular man with
crisp, hundred-dollar bills can fulfill her
desires, desires he, at one time could*
have fulfilled, but as her long-time*
partner, her husband still watches*
her behind closed eyes and she still
sits silently waiting for him to speak
to her, but never does.

Psychofairy | Faerie Whispers | poetry for the deep in heart | 41

Adult for Hire

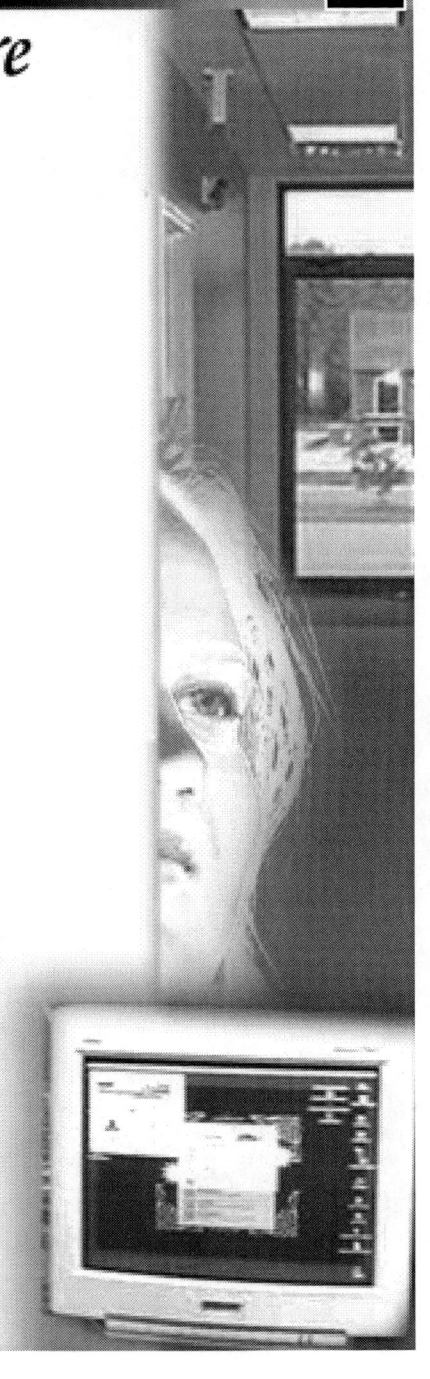

It doesn't matter what they say -
you're a kid in an adult world
making the green stuff, mailing the bills
they're adults in an adult world
and they're used to it
you are the new, fresh eyes
in the industry
they resent

It doesn't matter what they think
you're much younger
doing better, working harder,
holding the temper.
Look at them as they watch you
scroll their faces
imagine their burn
you're too young for this success

It doesn't matter how they act
you know which people notice you
which ones who prefer laughter
and which ones like a stick up their ass
they go to parties
cause you're the little baby
who can't go
watch their smiles
as they leave you with work loads
how will the toddler stand it?
it only matters that you do

The American Dream

I had a dream of black
and white
living together in harmony.
Racial equality and unity
would bring us close.
Martin Luther King Jr. said it best.
Protests, discrimination, and
demonstrations tore us further apart.
It was a difficult time to live in -
children fought with their teachers
parents fought with their children
children fought with their parents
everybody fought with everybody.
Where has the American dream gone?
National guard controlled
riots and mobs.
What would have happened without them?
People fought Vivian Malone unmercifully -
who was there to protect?
The footsteps of Rosa Parks
forced from her seats haunts us all.
Jane Pittman showed courage
drinking from the forbidden fountain.
What have we learned from the sixties?
George Wallace's segregation?
or have we behaved like our forefathers?
The parents set the examples -
we just follow their footsteps.
Some marched to show integration was right.
We, too can stop the violence.
We, Generation X, can lead the way.

Psychofairy — Faerie Whispers | poetry for the deep in heart

The Soul of a snow globe

The dancing has stopped -
they'll resume again.
Every mouth is frozen
like the base of an ice skating rink,
but it's not cold.
There is no movement -
not the slightest wiggle of a toe.
The trees in the background
are topped with white,
but it isn't snowing.
Each person is trapped
like the road block at an intersection -
they aren't trying to leave.
They look happy
though they aren't smiling.
It's the typical life
in an unshaken snow globe
where nobody has feelings or desires
and no one has thoughts that burn
with hatred and nobody worries about
tomorrow's deadlines or yesterday's absence,
but when it is shaken,
the violence begins
as the snow falls
like life on earth when
real thoughts begin
and dreams end.

44 Psychofairy | Faerie Whispers | poetry for the deep in heart

His Cheek

I can feel his cheek next to mine

soft, yet course

smooth, yet masculine

he seems so gentle

and thoughtful with his touch

I can smell his cologne

that wonderful scent of a man

trapping me like bait

pulling me in

Psychofairy   Faerie Whispers | poetry for the deep in heart

Undeniably Real

You watch her drench her shirt with morning snot
as she snuggles a seemingly large
caboose in your bucket seat.
It's not everyday you pick
up the girls at the bus stop,
but this one was different
she was real
undeniably real
and that's what makes you sick
sick enough to stare at her
as though you're human
while she leans there
running her dirty fingers
through her clean hair.
Is it so wrong to look
at a woman and expect nothing?
For once, not expect
a smile or a flopping tit,
just a plain old human
who wants a ride to work

Psychofairy

Faerie Whispers | poetry for the deep in heart

Thank God I'm Free

I used to lace my curls in pigtails,
but the older men thought I was childish,
a young prodigy trying to live a dream.
But while they pranced around in Camaros
and champagne-colored BMWs,
I would lean by the windows,
with my cheeks pressed to glass
and wish I were in the seat beside them
picking CDs and adjusting the air,
but I guess those guys were comfortable
with their hoods down and visors up,
their brunette locks twirling -
because their music was chosen
and black coffee already stirred
by an older lady too mature to smile
and too broken-in for new experiences.

I no longer hesitate to put on my
Garfield slippers with leather soles
or play with my lower lip in the mirror.
I don't blush anymore when they catch
me dancing to elevator music or
humming to the sound of a cash register.
In fact, sometimes I'm hoping they're
around the corner so I can talk to myself
and act surprised to see them.
Although I find them physically irresistible,
from now on, my eyes will focus
on someone who isn't past their prime.

Psychofairy   Faerie Whispers | poetry for the deep in heart   **47**

The mirror is punishment

a painful hour of camouflaging bruises

with concealer and powder

scars above my eyes

hide behind bangs and sunglasses

rouge disguises slashmarks on cheeks

I miss laughing at horror films -

now I am starring in them

buried beneath covers

trying not to breathe loudly

The phone cord reminds me of

rope used when wrists were tied to tables

even nail clippers on my dresser

remind me of cold scissors

that would run down my back

but when the bruises clear

maybe the memories will too

and I can gain strength

to walk outside

Fallen Petal

Psychofairy

Faerie Whispers | poetry for the deep in heart

Tell-Tale Book

The darkness gets darker
as horror fiction creeps
into the novel I read.
Long stories describing
evil doings leave me
with goose bumps and
spine-shreaking shrills.
My hair stands on end
like static, which leaves my
neck ever so cold --
and the book is still not finished.
I throw the book underneath my pillow
and rest on top,
trying to forget the last chapter,
but I can't.
So I hear a thump...thump...thump...
the book's heartbeat.
Thump! Thump! Thump!
It gets louder and louder
thumpety thump thump thump...
it gets softer and softer...
until silence.
I must have smothered it.

Psychofairy   Faerie Whispers | poetry for the deep in heart   **49**

Emvroidered Linen

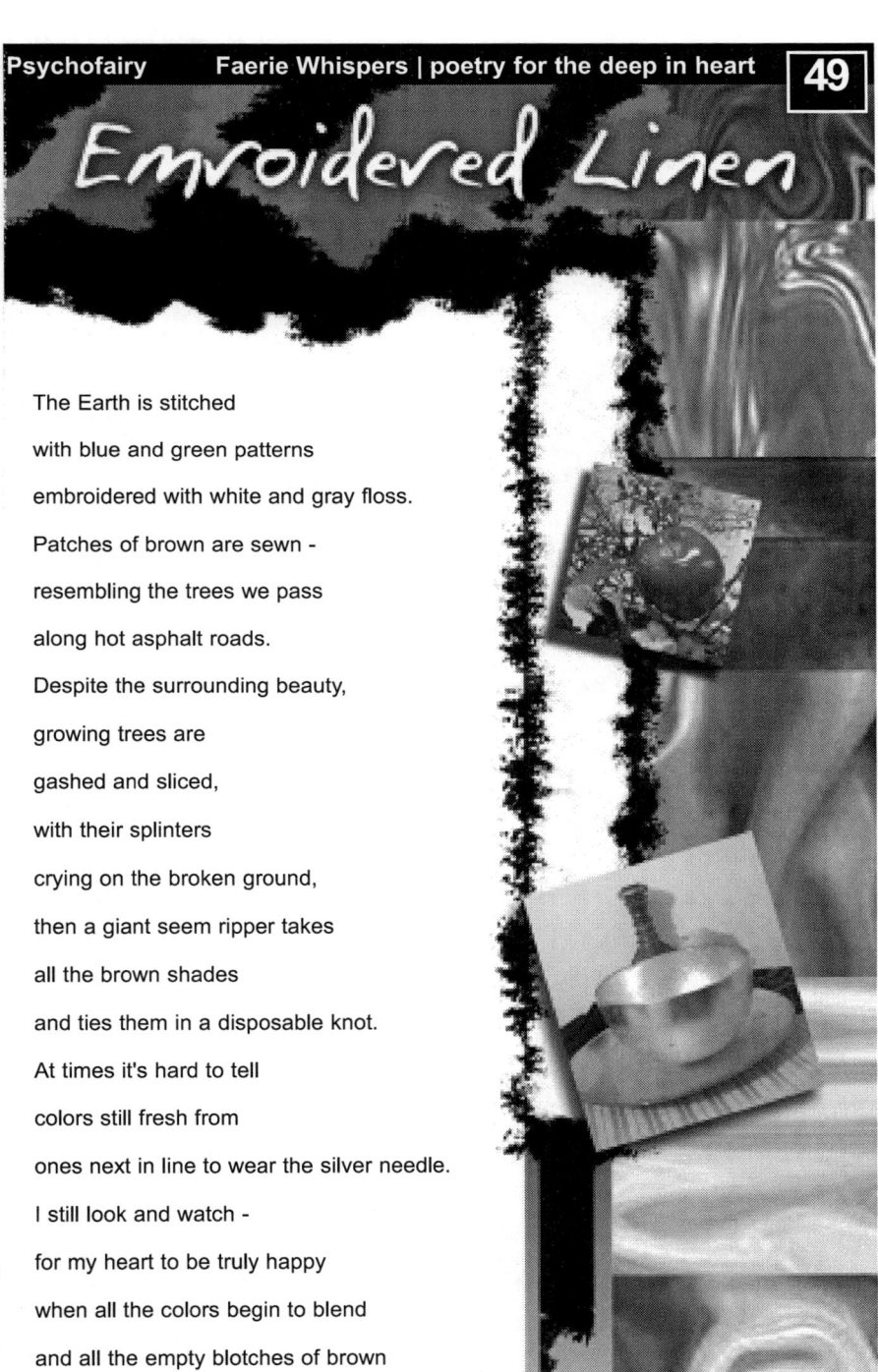

The Earth is stitched

with blue and green patterns

embroidered with white and gray floss.

Patches of brown are sewn -

resembling the trees we pass

along hot asphalt roads.

Despite the surrounding beauty,

growing trees are

gashed and sliced,

with their splinters

crying on the broken ground,

then a giant seem ripper takes

all the brown shades

and ties them in a disposable knot.

At times it's hard to tell

colors still fresh from

ones next in line to wear the silver needle.

I still look and watch -

for my heart to be truly happy

when all the colors begin to blend

and all the empty blotches of brown

can be resewn.

50 Psychofairy
Faerie Whispers | poetry for the deep in heart

Clay

for Clay Koontz, a flirtatious drunken poet

A giant sized poetic maniac

beer gurgling and never making sense

plastered to the point of insanity.

He says he is all love, and I don't doubt it!

A man of such greatness

has lots of romance in there. I've seen it.

He's always laughing, but at least he has teeth

He's always drinking - but never milk --

yet his body tastes sooo good. MMMM!

He talks to ladies' answering machines

and answers people's stupid questions...

he's a one of a kind ... a hunkish freak with a

squiggly on his arm representing his

undying love for me

and tattoos where the sun don't shine....

Oh come on, Clay -- we both saw them

last night was great. It was ALL good.

Don't deny it. I'm the best there was.

Fulfill me one last time.

Take my breath away.

I look forward to hearing your voice

on MY answering machine!

Clay 2

Clay never called my answering machine
where did I go wrong?
Was I too young for him?
Did he want a woman of legal drinking age?
He thinks he can just forget
our fling ever happened,
but it's not that easy,
I have feelings too!
He can't just throw me a non-alcoholic drink
and tell me to get over it.
He has to throw me some chocolate too!
He needs to hold on tight to the reigns
because my trail is a bit hilly.

Oh, come on Clay, we both know
you don't kiss me like you used to.
It's like you're John Wayne, and I'm your horse.
You can't just pet my belly
or kiss my mouth, then spit.
You can't ask for a piggy back ride
during dinner....
you gotta put your beer down first
and play with me!

Cotton
(for my husband)

There is freedom in your arms
humble and discreet
that enchants and holds me
just for a minute --
needing to feel wanted.
To feel skin
your pores and hair
and the sweat that melts your back.
I feel important in your arms.
Do not speak
Do not whisper
because our thoughts
are already aware
and my ears will only hear
the cotton of your shirt rubbing mine
No tribulations around
think only of this
our hands, our limbs
entwined like sheets --
there is freedom in your arms
and I hope you feel mine.

Psychofairy   Faerie Whispers | poetry for the deep in heart   53

fingers

his fingers were a saltwater lake,
soothing from afar,
but filthy on your skin.

discreetly hurting

Right now my stomach hurts
but still I lay on it
hoping my weight will fade the pain
I'm a little scared
a little anxious
and overwhelmed.
Pills taking their places
for Thursday night
when we attempt to add
a member to our lonely home.
Again,
If only the hot flashes would stop.
If only I could talk freely.
If only everyone around me
would stop flaunting their
perfect, fertile pregnancies,
then maybe my stomach
would feel a whole lot better.

| 54 | Psychofairy | Faerie Whispers | poetry for the deep in heart

Strings of a Guitar

My suitcase and guitar
in one hand
my music and pick
in the other
craving the long lost
corners of San Jose
to sit beside
shades of green
street signs
playing hymns from
a church book
listening to high heels
on concrete
watching women
with too much money,
dropping quarters
in my guitar case --
the coins rolling
on lined red velvet.
If only there was a
San Jose corner
here, I could afford
a new pick.

Seattle

Round skyscrapers
that chisel clouds
design their own reflections
off nearby ponds.
Three-story fountains
spurt in glassy bursts,
splashing the wind
and sharing the air,
unbelievable beautiful
sparkling even a
sleeping patch of water.
To see such a spherous
and mirrorous building
behind such a marvelous
and magnificent fountain,
it feels like watching
a glaze covering a painting
and the only way to
see the paint
is to turn off the water.

Psychofairy — Faerie Whispers | poetry for the deep in heart

He stands there
yapping away
like a hyper auctioneer
talking so fast
the micromachine guy
can't understand him,
walking, talking, rocking
back and forth
breathing, wheezing
overload to the lungs
puffing, huffing
blowing up a storm
exhale, no inhale
air not a must -
amazing behaving
leaving me waving,
but he never sees -
speaking, teaching
not meeting this man
who moves, soothes,
and puts on the grooves
but jumps, humps, and
gives me goosebumps
as I sit with a kit
biting my lower lip
nodding yes, yes, yes
don't stop yet
raising stew, goo,
and kalamazoo
with smoke from his nose
fire-breathing
birth-conceiving and
heart-beating irregularly
taking, making, faking
his speech
going stale, pale
it's hard to tell
when he'll ever inhale!

Psychofairy — Faerie Whispers | poetry for the deep in heart

Kryptonite

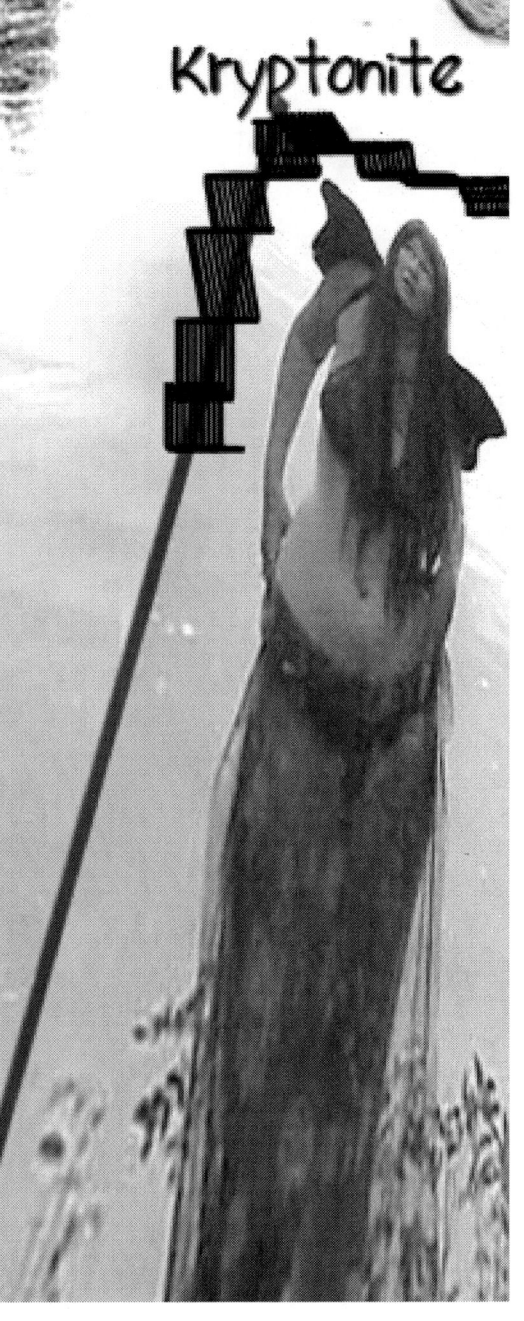

Beautiful women

with tanned faces

and content expressions

wake up happy

beside hunky firemen

that have poles

a foot long and

an ashtray wide,

unbelievably perfect

in the sight of

young girls maturing.

Clunky high heels

and shape tugging

pantyhose that trace

contours of long, luscious legs

then I think of those

broad-shouldered firemen

who are thinking

no matter how

beautiful their women are,

they want someone else

because they are

tired of crap

Psychofairy | Faerie Whispers | poetry for the deep in heart

Tunnel Vision

Oversized pumps, orange makeup, gaudy pearls
all my fantasy as a dreaming 8-year-old,
pretending to marry a horse-riding Robin Hood.
I would hum the march as I'd walk down,
smiling at the audience with a proud grin.

Barefoot, light face, small diamonds,
all my final reality as an emotional 19-year old
eyeing my knight and his three men,
music playing unnoticed as I tiptoed down,
feeling the eyes of a hundred guests.

Scared grin, shy smile, trembling hands
I could almost feel my father let go,
and he had waited for this moment
before I was even born.

Maturity makes a woman
Love makes a sweetheart
Spirit makes a lady
and I have become all three

Psychofairy   Faerie Whispers | poetry for the deep in heart   59

Bud's Dry

A cold beer sweats

leaving his manhood

dripping below his rim.

He sits there waiting

for lips to wrap

around his small hole

so he can exhale

a sigh of relief --

oh, the sweet release.

No more months of solitude

waiting to be manually thawed

this beer has been swallowed.

I Saw It

I was driving down 231

late one Wednesday night

a little cranky from work

a little sore from chairs

a little dreary from

car-filled cigarette smoke

and I saw it --

right above the new traffic light

flying, flashing, flirting

no stops, no fill-ups, no hello

just a visit

and for once...

I looked up,

ignoring the fact my brights

were blinding other drivers

I just stared.

A glimpse -

and this time

it was me who saw it

so I don't need professors

to convince me otherwise

Cedar Chest

That cedar chest is still

bolted to the floor

with denim sneaking out

like beads

off a counter

Initials you carved

with your pocketknife

stare at me

as my fingers rub them

Your aqua eyes

still dwell

in this room

haunting now

I want to stab

those gashed initials

because they aren't mine

but I'm too forgiving, too weak.

Psychofairy

Dear Son
I learned how to play piano this week
hoping that when you're conceived
you'll have mastered a talent
by the time you're spewed in this
insanely cold world
brave enough to try
Chariots of Fire with your mighty fingers

It's been five days since
I've cursed, I think.
Maybe that will make you pure
If I wear small shoes
maybe your feet won't
be as big as mine and maybe your toes
won't be ingrown or smelly.

I cleaned up my car yesterday
maybe one day I'll pay you
to clean it for me.
But I'd like to be the one to show you...
run our hands in circles over paint
trade our cloths and rags,
race each other to the water hose.

It's been two hours since
I've though about you last,
wondering if you were asleep
or watching Johnny Quest cartoons
or if daddy was feeding you
our leftover manicotti...
but I bet right now you're sleeping
with your eyes fluttering to a dream
learning how to play
piano with your feet.

Alive

I fell in love with you
all over again today
and all I did was open my eyes

STAGEFRIGHT

It feels like spiders
crawling on my neck
those little feet
inching across my skin

like the sound of howling dogs
in the middle of the night --
it seems to go away

as long as I'm nervous
those spiders will keep me shaking
no matter how often
I scratch my neck
or stand by a heater,
my showers will always be there...
and they will
keep haunting me
until showtime.

Psychofairy Faerie Whispers | poetry for the deep in heart 65

Quick Game of Chess

He has his mind
written on his face.
The pleasure of glorious
victory express
his feelings.
He smiles, knowing
he'll win again.
My weakness is clear;
always defensive.
I stare at him and
watch his next move
like a cat would
a butterfly as it flutters
its glassy wings.
He peers up,
knowing I lost,
and we laugh,
then sigh,
good game he says,
shaking my hand.

The Look of a poet

(for Kristin Kostick)

She looks like a poet
with black, spiral curls dangling
in her face uncontrollably
like overgrown weeds in a garden.
She dresses like a poet
with long, flowing, flowery shirts
and mismatched skirts that
hug her ankles.
The window sill is her friend
as she sits with her tired elbows
propped on her knees,
reading a romance novel
about a soldier gone to war.
She refuses the title of poet,
yet she speaks only metaphors -
no matter what the topic.
She is a bird that
denies its wings
yet soars gracefully through the sky
taking flight to a foreign land.
She looks meek
like a female Picasso
and clearly seeks confused
thoughts and arranges them
into colors and shades
until carefully printed on paper.
She just has that LOOK...
the look of a poet.

Faerie Whispers | poetry for the deep in heart

Confidence

He marched past women
with admiring eyes and full smiles;
wedding rings tucked in their pockets.
He didn't notice
but he saw
old clothes I was folding
beside rumbling washing machines.
I sensed a bit of jealousy
from those wide-eyed ladies
with slender figures and new outfits
because he found a plain girl
with shaking hands
hidden behind stained socks...
walls of my mouth
felt hotter than irons when he said,
"I'll meet you at your house when you're done."
I watched his thin body
stroll to his car,
followed by a dozen female feet
trampling the frail carpet like children,
to peek from the nearest window.
I felt like the big girl at prom
when the king pulls her in for a dance
while skinny blondes raise their noses.
I wanted to jump and swing my hair
to prove I was their equal
but knew if I pretended,
their eyes would grow greener
so I grabbed the remains from the table,
yawned, and closed the door.
I went to my gold truck
and barely pressed the gas
until I was around the corner.
I floored it until black smoke
blinded my sideview mirrors.
He was leaning on his car
when I pulled into my pebbled driveway.
It took a while to figure out
how he knew where I lived,
till I remembered telling him weeks before.
I looked around,
hoping those lusting women
that once huffed at me
could see I won
a genuine, clean-cut man
who held my like soft linen.

you've watched me over the years
all those years,
even the ones we tried to forget,
and I still turned out all right.
I know I've messed up a couple times,
maybe more than I admit
but you continue to forgive
yes, I've snuck out in your truck
returned it without gas
and made you late for work,
I've hidden the remote control
so you'd bribe me with money
to return it
and I even made long distance
phone calls and you paid for them.
You've had twelve years to prepare for a teenager
and when you got one,
you realized it would take years more.
but, I, too, should have been prepared
should've learned from my mistakes
before they would involve you
like getting suspended -
you paying for my summer school,
that was vacation money
you saved for months.
I know college is right around the block
but I still have more to learn.
I'd rather learn about adulthood
through eyes that have watched me,
someone like you who knows
how much money I must earn
to buy all the alarm clocks I need
and everything else you notice
that I never do.
Dad, thank you,
you handled me better than I would have.

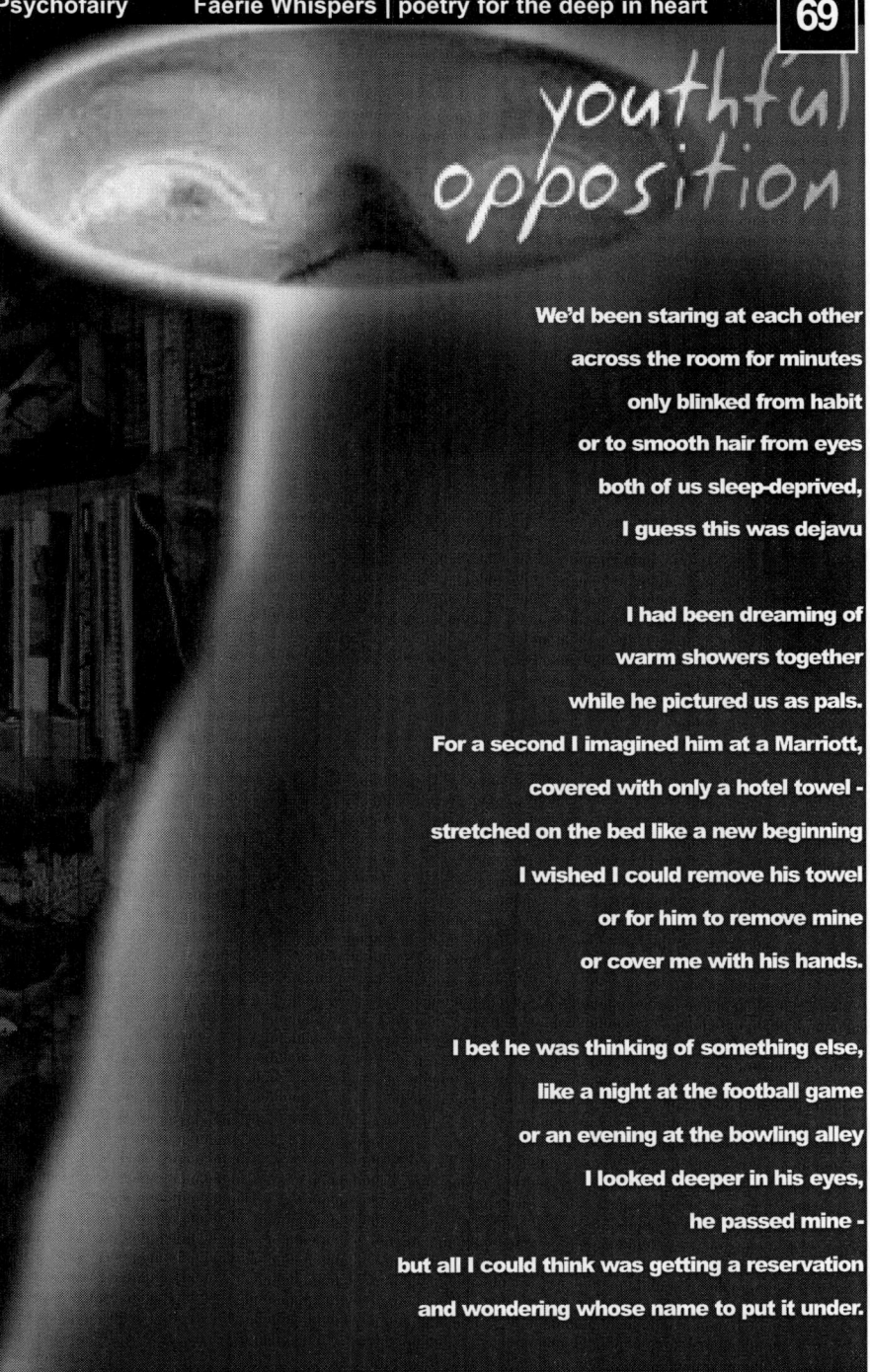

youthful opposition

We'd been staring at each other
across the room for minutes
only blinked from habit
or to smooth hair from eyes
both of us sleep-deprived,
I guess this was dejavu

I had been dreaming of
warm showers together
while he pictured us as pals.
For a second I imagined him at a Marriott,
covered with only a hotel towel -
stretched on the bed like a new beginning
I wished I could remove his towel
or for him to remove mine
or cover me with his hands.

I bet he was thinking of something else,
like a night at the football game
or an evening at the bowling alley
I looked deeper in his eyes,
he passed mine -
but all I could think was getting a reservation
and wondering whose name to put it under.

Psychofairy — Faerie Whispers | poetry for the deep in heart

I Just Walked Away

Five months of blissful
and overwhelming sweetness
erased from time,
swallowing the guilt
and forgiving the fights
seems so simple on paper
feels like feet on fallen shards
and even though my toes
are bleeding from the cuts
I know they always heal
but the floor we walked
may never be repaired.

Psychofairy   Faerie Whispers | poetry for the deep in heart   71

The Drunk Man Who Stunk

It was obvious he was drunk
maybe not staggering
but definitely plastered
he was wearing a Budweiser hat
made from red styrofoam,
the same stuff used to make
sun visors at fundraisers -
but he was drinking a Zima...
He raised his chilled,
half-filled bottle
to give his new year's toast
and a kid with a wine bottle
said "CHEERS!"
but before they could drink,
their bottles collided
like Harding and Kerigan
and broke

in half
and the crowd stood silent
watching
waiting
to approve their reaction.
But the drunk man,
an old guy in New York
from Alabama,
began to laugh,
his huge belly
rolling like bubble gum
in his drenched overalls
while the young kid
began to cry.

Psychofairy

Faerie Whispers | poetry for the deep in heart

Magazine Movement

He called after eleven
when the wet violet paint on my toe-nails
were drying above some piled pillows.
An erotic advice column in Cosmo
spread-eagled on my bed
as I curiously read about keeping men happy

He greeted me with three hellos,
then asked how my day went
and I told him his lips made me crazy
He asked if I had Tori Amos' latest album
and I told him he was gorgeous

I could hear him smiling
as I fumbled past Neutrogena ads
to samples of Obsession
where I slid my wrists against scented strips,
wishing he could smell it

I probably could,
through the little dots in the phone.
Magazines cluttered my room
like bacteria on Biore pads
but I think he knew
that I knew
each Cosmo and Glamour I read for him

He stopped chatting for a minute
and we sat in silence.
I, interested in a new Q and A
he, probably looking at the ceiling
talked without words
and it felt interesting
until Cosmo said we were insecure.

Psychofairy   Faerie Whispers | poetry for the deep in heart   73

Drunk Fish

Laying out beside the pool

at a Massachusetts hotel,

throwing pennies in the water

for children to find,

I notice the whirlpool turns

like a dozen fish in alcohol.

| 74 | Psychofairy | Faerie Whispers | poetry for the deep in heart |

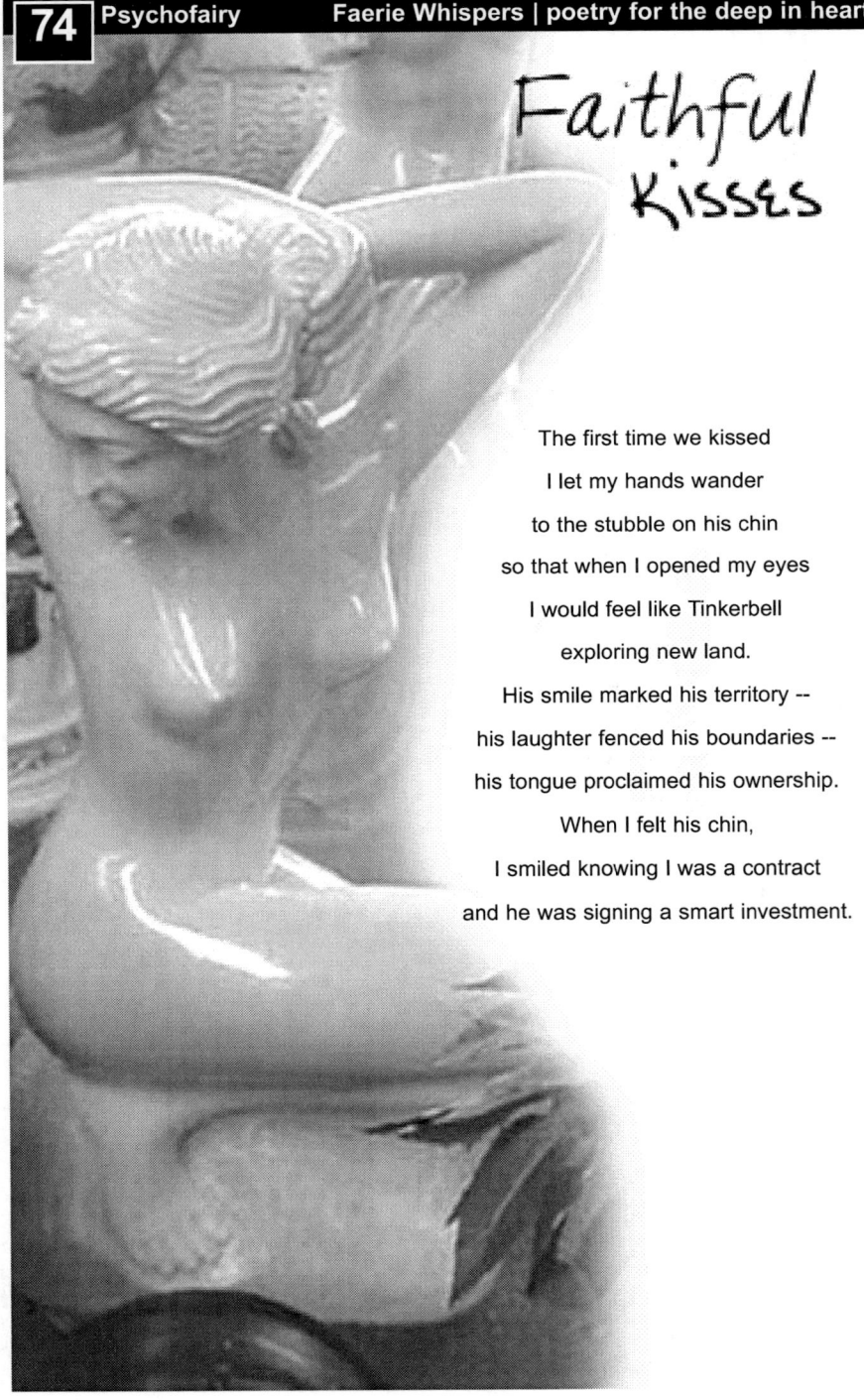

Faithful Kisses

The first time we kissed
I let my hands wander
to the stubble on his chin
so that when I opened my eyes
I would feel like Tinkerbell
exploring new land.
His smile marked his territory --
his laughter fenced his boundaries --
his tongue proclaimed his ownership.
When I felt his chin,
I smiled knowing I was a contract
and he was signing a smart investment.

Throwing Fire

I could tell she was hurting
and so was I,
but it didn't change anything.
The same chronic words,
the same fatal expressions,
the same deadly silence at the end.
We could scream for hours
about buying the wrong kind of bread
or taking two peppermints from the banker.
Sometimes I sit and wonder
what the ultimate insult would be,
but realize each word is equal
and that if maybe we shout compliments
we can go to sleep with laughter.

Our Hands, A Refuge

I like those days
when you place
your sweaty hands in mine
or sometimes
when you're cold
I know the warmth of my palms
can be your heater.

I even like those nights
when we shiver together
in the same coat
or spend minutes talking about who's colder.

But I know
in stormy weather,
when you're running away from raindrops,
you'll place your delicate hands in a jacket
and I'll be your warm pocket.

The Cure for Loneliness

I have this friend who flies

from boyfriend to boyfriend

by the Fridays,

meeting the grunge

and even clean-cut

khaki strutters,

but I've been known for

longer relationships

so I shocked the both of us

when I farewelled my fiance

and roomed with her.

It was all his fault, of course,

but I still missed his kisses

and occasional hugs.

She told me to forget him

and meet someone else --

a southern gentleman with jade eyes

and an aqua soul.

I now feel the warmth

of gently hands on hot skin,

cool fingers on a trembling heart --

and when he holds me,

I know I've clipped my wings

because this fairy is not flying anywhere.

Psychofairy   Faerie Whispers | poetry for the deep in heart

The Innocence of a Man

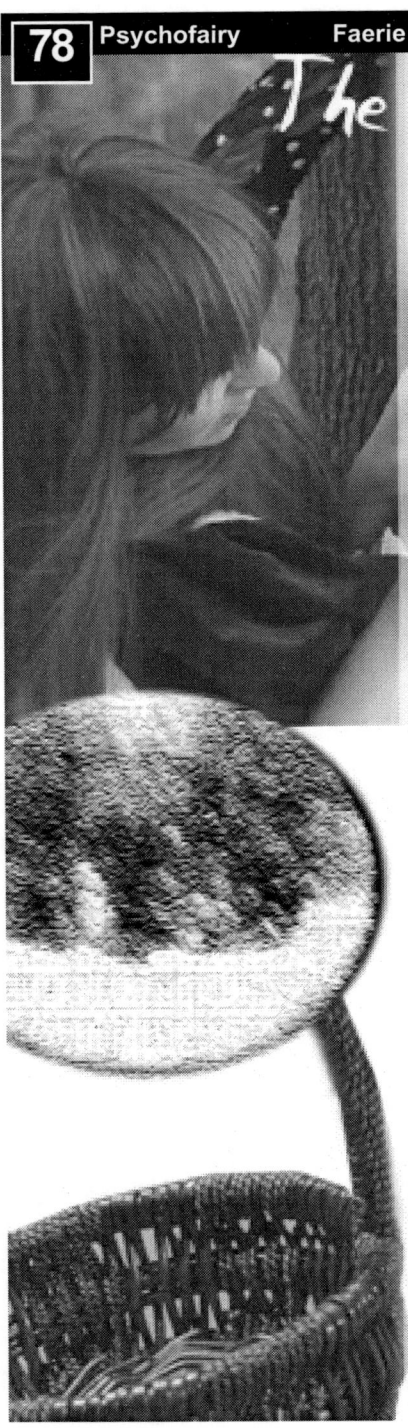

It was a bit strange
sitting beside him
as he was always sure to keep his head up
and shuffle his feet in his chair.
I used to watch him
play with his chin and jaw,
massaging the hard stubs of hair
that irritated his thoughts.
I can't see him anymore,
just hear him -
listening for each breath
that blows his bangs up when he's hot.
He likes to fidget with his face,
as though he's feeling it
with the innocence of a sealed box.
He could do a lot with his hands,
now pink and peach from the cold,
but he holds just a pen,
instead of clinging to his hair,
not frizzled from the weather like mine.
His eyes change with the clouds,
altering moods with his expressions,
each ocean seems to float with his heart,
but if you ask him to smile, he tries not to.
He slouches into his chair,
but his posture still remains.
How can a man that beautiful...sit
When all I can think about is
standing beside him,
hoping he knows I'm there -
How can a man that bright...smile
When all I can think about is
falling into his shadow,
hoping he'll catch me -
How can a man that sweet...talk
When all my words get tongue-tied
and I wonder if anything came out,
when he can just sit there quietly
with nothing on his mind -
except a few thoughts of some chic
but I still sit in my little space
watching him play with his jaw
hoping maybe he'll tilt his head
towards me.

Psychofairy

Faerie Whispers | poetry for the deep in heart

The ghosts of beer bottles and
wine coolers filter the air
as I squeeze between crowds.
The spirits of potato chips and
broken Doritos sifts through the
ground
below the wet, dark streets,
now stained with urine.
I feel shackled, but have no chains -
yet know I am locked in my own
financial prison of stolen luxuries.
I am the one taking money
from deep, leather jackets,
ignoring the screams of old women
and moans and grunts from young
men
who realize their pockets
have been emptied.
Haunting stares search Times Square,
eager to find the culprit -
but everyone looks alike.
All are plastered with their eyes plant-
ed
on the flashing Sphere of New Years -
ready to watch it fall, fall, fall,
fall like a corpse in a graveyard.
Each arm that waves at a camera and
each blue scarf that sways to the sky
seems like a rotten bone with batter-
ies -
with barely enough energy -
buried beneath a black surface.
Shimmering watches and
glittering bracelets
shine on wrists under
blinding street lamps -
pure, golden, and valued.
I walk with a bounce of charisma
like I am rain
fluttering on fresh petals
leaving lavender shadows on the
ground.
But in real life there are no violet
scents,
only a trail of misty eyes in moonlight.
The only thing that chimes
are the voices of drag queens
leaning on a wall of a
Chinese restaurant and
the only thing that clings
are the chilled Michelob mugs
when people give their
toasts and resolutions.
I float by a man who is nestled
in his girlfriend's chest,
reach into his coat,
expecting to grasp something expen-
sive,
but all I feel is a wet, Winston ciga-
rette
it's burnt ash dissolving in my palm.
My feet skid and slide,
but I can't feel them -
like my pick-pocketing is
leading me towards
the Asylum, Bellevue.
I look to that ball of lightning fury
one last time
9-8-7
close my eyes and lean my head back
6-5-4
press my lips together and kiss the air
3-2-1
...will this really be a happy new year?

Hush Hush Darling

He cradles her like a child
and her tear-stricken face is molded in his chest.
He's been holding her for hours
and she hasn't moved.
Tears still stream from her
bloodshot eyes and she sniffles
softly with the slightest sounds.
He's tired of holding her
but she's comfortable
and he doesn't want to be insensitive.
She mumbles something about marriage,
but he didn't catch it,
so he whispers "I don't know"
because it answers every question.
She begins to cry louder,
but he doesn't notice,
so he continues to hold her
cuddling her
as he stares at the dotted ceiling
listening to her peaceful breaths.

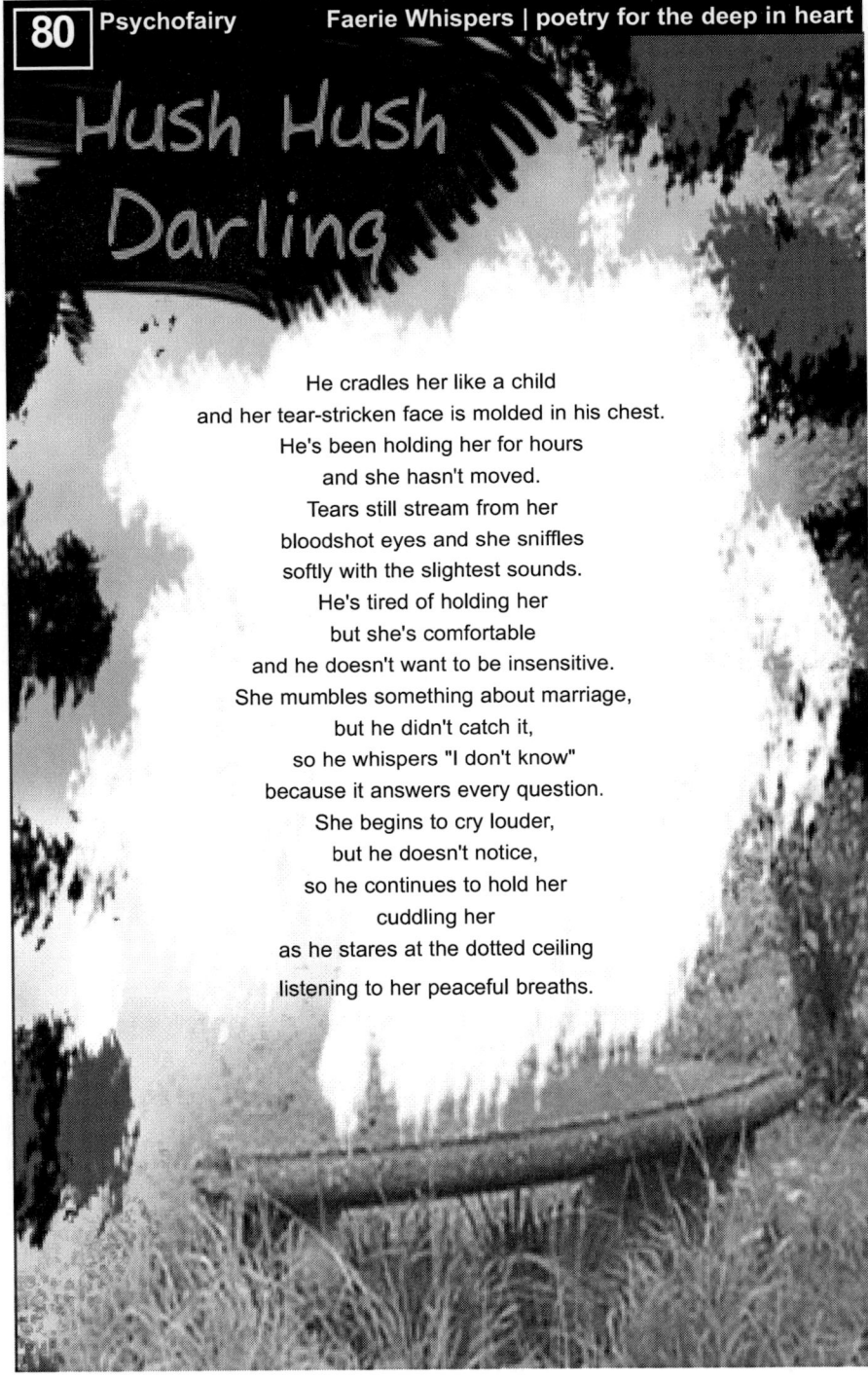

A Toast

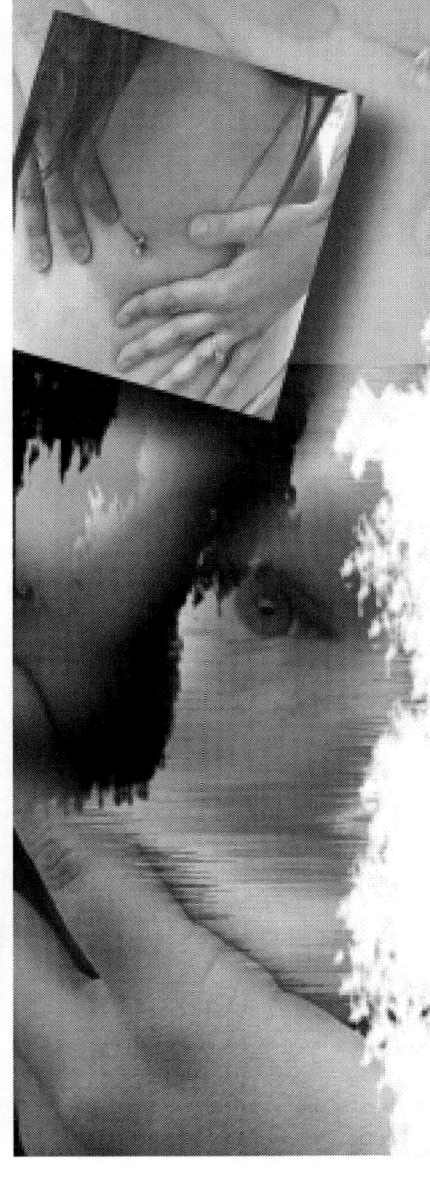

I'd like to make a toast
dear daughter
that you hold beauty
beyond your fifties
that your hands
enjoy the feel of pens
of writing and sketching
that your attire
stay stylish and pressed
clean and coordinated
that your laughter
be genuine and free,
contagious to others,
that your mind
learn easily and
hold memories longer
that when you grow
you share with others
your knowledge, belongings
memories and works
and your clothes
be passed down
to the next miracle

Cliques

She would weep wearily

in her own recluse,

so challenged by the world,

the only letters she scrawled

were to herself.

No little old ladies ever tapped

at her door with fruit baskets

or handmade pound cakes,

just the wind howling

on new hinges.

This town never welcomed her.

They would shop in sunlit bazaars

and thundering temples of trinkets,

but never invited her.

Even I would travel in cliques,

my own little foursome,

where no visitors could peak.

And yet when I go home,

I cry when no visitors knock on my door.

Psychofairy Faerie Whispers | poetry for the deep in heart

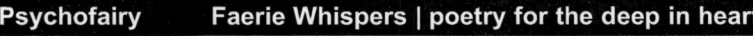

she just kept hitting me
over and over
and I was screaming so loud
more I cried
the more she would hit
and it burned like fire
could I have just not been born
would that solve her problems?
me being fat, eating too much
hit me for that
hit me for talking back, disagreeing
sometimes hit me 100 times in a row
leave so many bruises, marks -
I would look in the mirror after it was over
examine my butt, always fearing the worst
always red, sometimes blue
sometimes bleeding
it would hurt so bad
I wanted to slap her with her own belts
and ten years later, I still feel this
still feel her hitting me as hard as she could
telling me I was the worst child
that I was going to hell
because I never read the Bible like her
and that I never prayed on my knees like her
and that I would turn out like a slut
because I kissed a boy
she would do this to my sister too
and she would put on 4 pairs of underwear
to numb the pain
but it never helped
I tried to take her beatings for her
she was so thin, so frail
I could stomach the pain
hold it in, wait for years
write about it

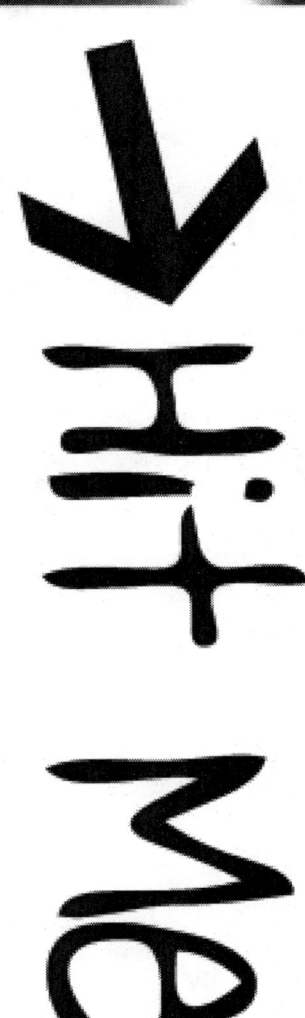

December

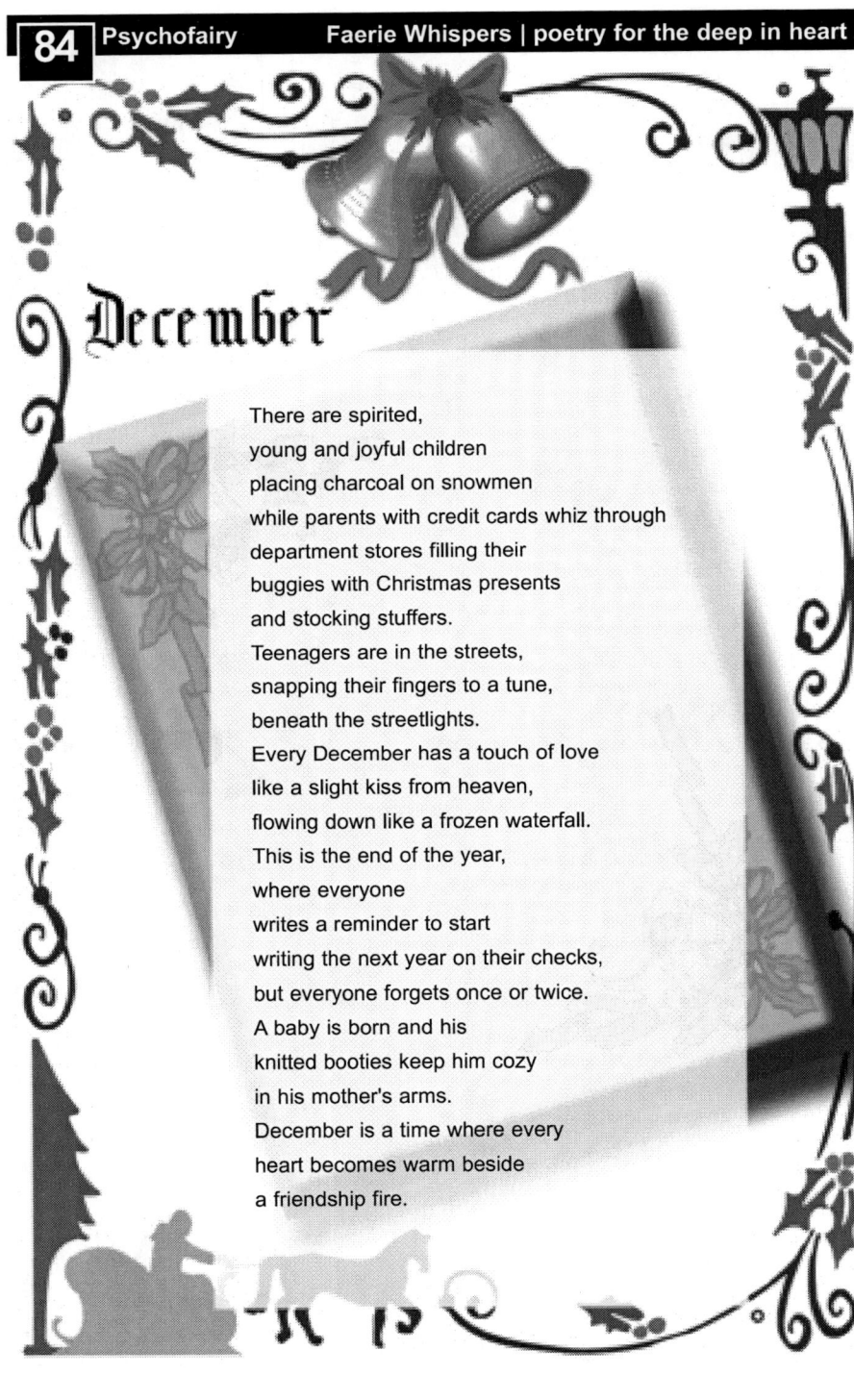

There are spirited,
young and joyful children
placing charcoal on snowmen
while parents with credit cards whiz through
department stores filling their
buggies with Christmas presents
and stocking stuffers.
Teenagers are in the streets,
snapping their fingers to a tune,
beneath the streetlights.
Every December has a touch of love
like a slight kiss from heaven,
flowing down like a frozen waterfall.
This is the end of the year,
where everyone
writes a reminder to start
writing the next year on their checks,
but everyone forgets once or twice.
A baby is born and his
knitted booties keep him cozy
in his mother's arms.
December is a time where every
heart becomes warm beside
a friendship fire.

Behind Clenched TEETH

That'll be seventeen dollars and three cents

I say, extending an empty palm toward

the slow customer, who fumbles through

her large, leather purse like a mother

digging through sand for an earring.

There are two screaming toddlers begging

for candy, but she just shakes her head.

They ask again, then begins to slap them -

on the legs, face,back

anywhere...to get them to be quiet.

I want to hit her,

so she'll know how it feels,

but I'm at work and

I have to respect her.

Don't hit your child, I think to myself,

not like that.

She gives me a crumbled bill

and snaps at her children like a bully

in elementary school.

I tear the receipt and give her the change.

Customers are always right, I remember.

Have a nice day, I say smiling -

hiding clenched teeth.

Just Because

I'm a rubberband

tangled in your hair

not moving or breathing while

your living-light flutters

like a fly glued to a frying pan.

I see you all around

but you only see me through

a mirror lost in your room

like that Fleetwood Mac tape

left unopened in your closet.

I'm a piggy-bank

you invest nothing in -

just sitting there on the floor

like a child left at daycare

without lunch or toys.

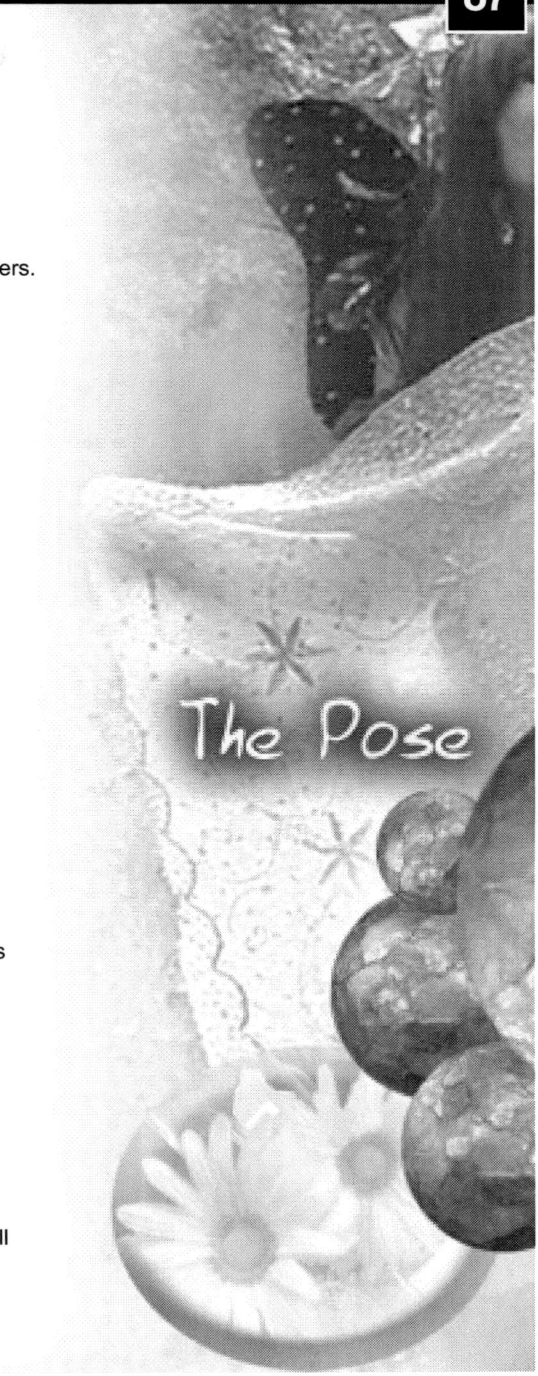

The Pose

She stands

upright and tall

like a high heel

supporting herself

with stands and hangers.

Her plastic face

shows no emotion,

yet her feelings

can almost be seen.

She's staring

off in space

with a blank mind

only filled with

air flowing

from one ear

to the other -

like other mannequins

posing with

no expressions.

I make a crazy face

but she can't see

I stand upright and tall

to let her know -

I can do it too.

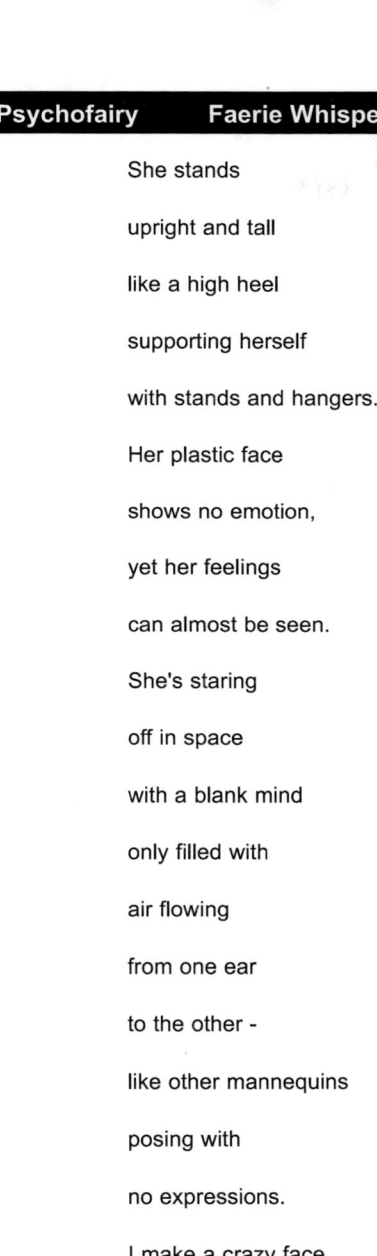

Peeping Tom

I saw guy -
a clean cut man
with a red shirt and wrinkle-free pants.
He unlocked his car
with a mile-long keychain -
sat inside,
rolled down the window,
looked in the mirror,
fixed his hair,
his teeth,
and his smile.
my lips curled up,
almost embarrassed to watch...
but curiosity set in
as he drummed the
steering wheel to the
beat of his radio.
I tried to hide a giggle
but I couldn't help it -
I ducked my head
as he faced my way,
too shy to face my victim;
yet as I knelt there
with my head buried
under the dashboard,
I began to imagine
someone else watching me
away from the parking lot.

Psychofairy — Faerie Whispers | poetry for the deep in heart

The Crush

He asks me my name

and I stand silent

He gives me a wink

and I freeze

He smiles

and I return it

He says hello

and I blush

I walk past him

and fall

hoping he'll save me.

Abduction

I should've been there
I should've seen it
but it can't re-occur
sighting after sighting
the smell of evil and terror
an inhuman voice full of greed

I should've been there
I should've heard them
but the yelps could no longer be cried
panicked people scream for peace
another attack leaves everyone breathless
yet they beg for the
torture to stop

I should've said something
I should've listened
but I would not believe
odd creatures would abduct
a frightened baby boy
from his newlywed mother's arms
to live in a land of nothingness

I should've been there
I should've gone too
but I was caught in traffic
so I had to hear about the
child's disappearance on the news
but nobody knew how he left

I should've said something
they should've listened
but most people just don't believe
and I didn't either
until I saw something
I should've never seen.

accident

Smog blocks my sight
as my car's headlights shine.
A big blur and a
white shadow
cover the atmosphere
as I turn on my blinker...
squinting my eyes
hoping to see
five hundred feet ahead,
I notice to my dismay
the car in front of me
is parked and I'm still going.

92 | Psychofairy
Faerie Whispers | poetry for the deep in heart

Little Sparrow

A brownish-gray sparrow
lies quietly on a brick ledge.
The sun bears on it,
forcing the creature to squint.
Its leg is wounded
with tiny ants wandering
near it with a hungered curiosity.
The poor thing can't move
with wings motionless
as my dropped jaw...
its face is the size of my thumb
and I cuddle it into my palm
and assure it things will be alright
even though the vet is closed
and I know I can't care for it...
so I walk it to a nearby park,
let it crawl slowly away from my hand
let it bury itself into brown grass
to wish its life away.

Psychofairy | Faerie Whispers | poetry for the deep in heart

Through the Eyes of a paraplegic

Listening

to muffled voices

not speaking a word

their laughter

is my sadness

my body

unable to walk

sits cross-legged

not crying

not thinking

just watching

expressions

of everyone who

feels sorry for me

Stress Reliever

I never really stared at a
bearded man before,
but last night I did.
He had pain in his eyes
and anguish on his lips.
Maybe family problems
placed them there.
His brownish-gray beard
was combed neatly south,
flirting comfortably around his chin.
He ran his palm through
his whiskers,
tweezing each hair with a
twirl of his finger...
it wouldn't look right if
I played with my chin like that.
His beard was his stress reliever,
always there for him,
but could one day disappear.
For his own sake,
should keep it,
so his pain
can be endured.

Psychofairy | Faerie Whispers | poetry for the deep in heart

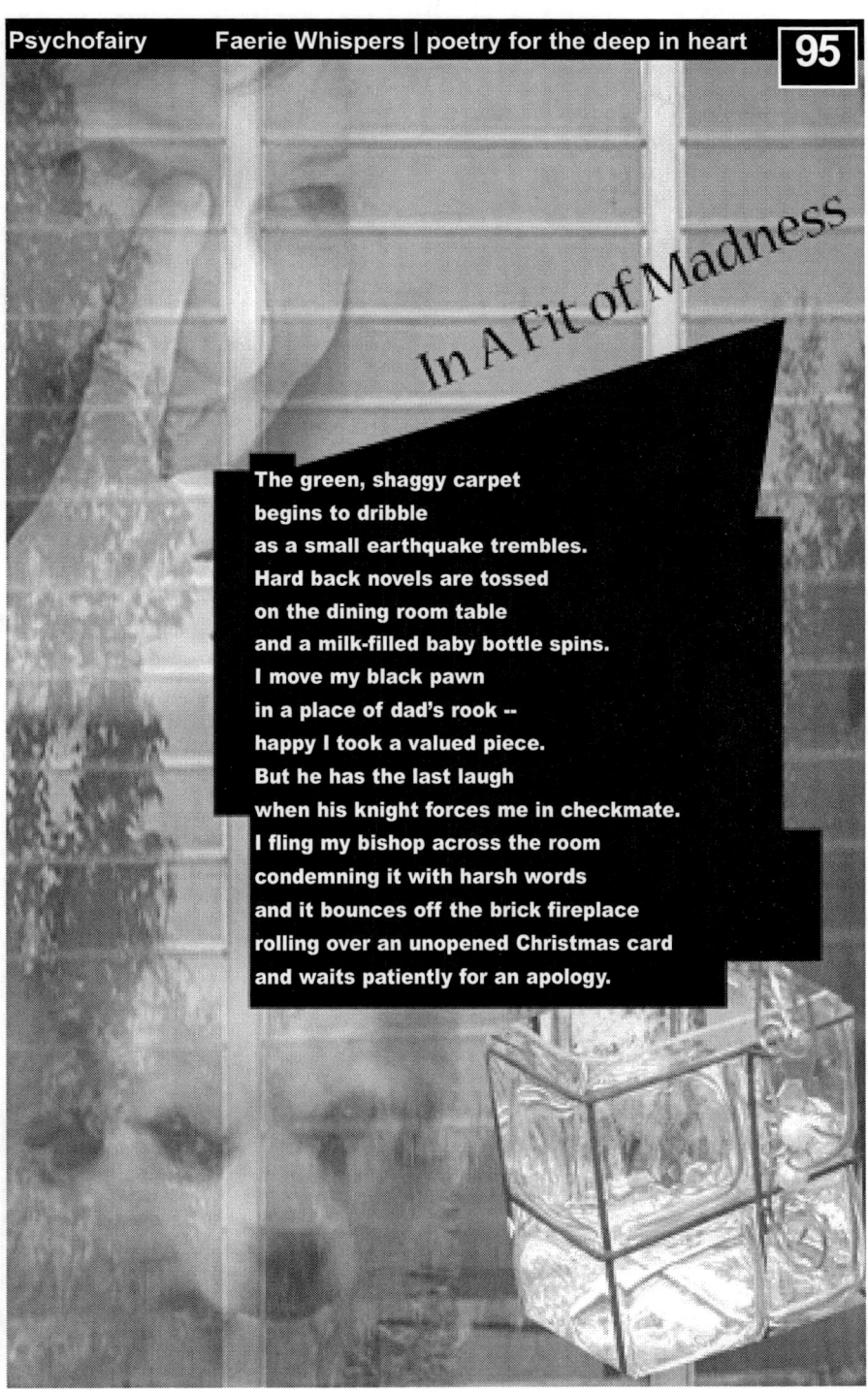

In A Fit of Madness

The green, shaggy carpet
begins to dribble
as a small earthquake trembles.
Hard back novels are tossed
on the dining room table
and a milk-filled baby bottle spins.
I move my black pawn
in a place of dad's rook --
happy I took a valued piece.
But he has the last laugh
when his knight forces me in checkmate.
I fling my bishop across the room
condemning it with harsh words
and it bounces off the brick fireplace
rolling over an unopened Christmas card
and waits patiently for an apology.

Psychofairy

Faerie Whispers | poetry for the deep in heart

Runaway Mother

Packing two old shirts and a ragged
pair of blue jeans into a white
satchel, the lady crawled
through her small bedroom window
and stepped out into the night with a
twenty-dollar bill in her pocket.
She walked down the dirt road
lined with mobile homes.
Her three kids were asleep -- sprawled
on a dirty, blue mattress.
Being a single mother wasn't easy,
and she wanted no more stress,
no more children to depend on her
no more babies to cry for milk
she loved her husband
but he didn't love her the same.
She got up, leaving as he did
leaving her kids
to be raised by some stranger
who felt sorry for them,
looks back, just one glance
never returns

You asked me what I learned

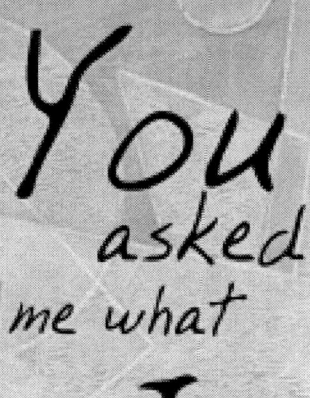

I learned how to handle trust,
the investment it has when you
lend it to the world
and the value it could have
if it is returned.

I learned that honesty is not only truth
but a promise in someone's eyes,
an unspoken pact stronger than words...
I learned that confiding secrets
can peace pain more than painting them
and the respect one earns when they listen.

Now I know who will hear
who will walk away
and who has listened before I even spoke.

Psychofairy — Faerie Whispers | poetry for the deep in heart

she smelled like candles

The lady browsed
through vanilla candles
smelling each one with eyes shut,
then tilted her head
as if she were fainting...
she was a large woman
with heavy thighs, thick ankles
and a pouting stomach
who smelled like cinnamon and oranges
and customers enjoyed her scent
as they squeezed to move around her.
She gazed up with her green eyes,
which almost reminded me of glazed marbles
on her puffy, yet porcelain face -
proving her more attractive than a "fat lady"
her beauty seeping through her clothes
like sunshine through clean lace.

Psychofairy   Faerie Whispers | poetry for the deep in heart

Invisible

I treated you invisibly
you never knew what to say
I saw your eyes grow anxious
but then I'd slowly walk away

did you ever think
that maybe I cared -
a little too much or a little less
just tell me you've
thought about me
so I don't have to guess

I'd hold you tight
if you'd let me
grab you tie
and yank you closer
trip your feet
to make you fall
with me --

did you ever think
that maybe I loved you,
I just didn't know it
at the time,
just let your heart
believe someone is mine.

Ready or Not

this morning in my father's golden truck,
while stopped at a traffic light,
my dad spoke about responsibility.
"One day you'll be out on your own,
and I want you to get you as ready as I can."
I laughed and said
I was ready now.
He shook his head quickly
like a father does,
when he knows he is right.
"You need to learn how to manage
your money," he said.
Telling him I'd hire an accountant,
he knew that I knew
he was right.
I was far from ready.

Psychofairy — Faerie Whispers | poetry for the deep in heart

for Amy

She stares at her bathroom mirror,

gazing at her haunting reflection.

She glides her lifeless fingers over

her pale, discolored cheeks,

now emerged in coldness.

Her eyes are unrecognizable

they just don't belong

She hears her temporary heartbeat and shudders.

This isn't happening

the doctors must be mistaken.

Morbid maladies can't happen

to people like me, she devised aloud

thinking back to an unforgettable night of lascivious desires,

she remembers her faults she'll eternally regret.

A one-night fling with booze with a man she met that morning -

Now she has to live with this endless worry and grief.

A life of despair, loneliness and self-abuse.

Panic and hopelessness overflow her empty soul

like the Pacific Ocean pouring into a

plastic measuring cup.

Now she loathes the son of a bitch

who the hell was he anyway?

Some guy at a mechanics shop who

offered to fix her tire for free...

he supplied her this passport to death

and she sobs at realizing this isn't a dream,

that no mechanic will ever offer

to patch up or fix the constant dripping

of her heart.

AIDS

Psychofairy — Faerie Whispers | poetry for the deep in heart

Eyes of Gray

His eyes are like the night,
deep, dark and black.
They are planets
with orbits and moons,
comets and stars
encircled around clouds.

Her eyes are like the day,
shallow, light and white.
The sun lies in her
and she glows with shine.
Tans and burns,
lined with bright colors.

The day and the night meet,
becoming a shade of gray.
No black holes or supernovas.
It is a pretty gray
like ashes from the sun
or craters of the moon.

Cats Under a tin roof

An old apartment building screamed

at me last Saturday,

one Dad and I lived in for years --

a place where we often laughed

at notorious neighbors with loud libidos.

I remembered each one,

including four sets of lesbians

who scratched those thin, tattered walls

like Freddy Kruger in a cat fight.

I couldn't help but hear

aroused ladies moaning

and plastic vibrators humming

but all I wanted to hear

was a burglar lurking

so he could steal their batteries.

Unfortunately, no burglar ever came,

but an arsenic did

and torched the top half of the house...

looking closely,

I can still see fingernails

forever on the windows

to be forgotten like old fantasies.

QUOTING THE MUTE VETERANS

With my loaded lenses and straightened
strap around my neck,
new notepad in palm,
persistent pen in fingers -
I hungered for a delicious headline.

The elderly crowd sat
listening to the veterans
and descendants of POWs in Vietnam,
cousins who were KIA in World War II,
great uncles buried with purple hearts
and brothers who had bad parachutes in Desert Storm.

I know nothing about war
nor anyone in a war
and I didn't know the man with the fatal parachute
but in this town where everybody is SOMEbody,
they do.

I could almost feel the crowd staring me down,
persuaded I was the paparazzi
exploiting their pain...
here I was, deaf to their mute voices,
staying unemotional and unfazed -
too professional to let their compelling experiences
actually settle in my heart
like the fiance who wrote the Dear John letter
to the man she knows will not survive.

I could hear the veterans' deep eyes murmur
as a survived pilot said these words,
"Veterans give freedom of press, not the media.
Veterans give freedom of speech, not heartless journalists."
I bowed my head in shame
because I was both.

You call me Lily,
but you treat me like a thorn.
I wish I were that flower on your cheek,
that golden petaled plant
stuck to your face.
I wish I were the soft melodies
in your head
the sweet sounding words that echo...
the sweet sounding words that sing...
but all you do
reminds me of a flower in the rain
bending over sideways,
never feeling any wind.
You always held me like a blanket -
I thought you gave a damn
but when you stencil holly on your window
and tiny berries on your door,
I think of mistletoe
dangling above the carpet
as I stand alone.

Flower on Your Face

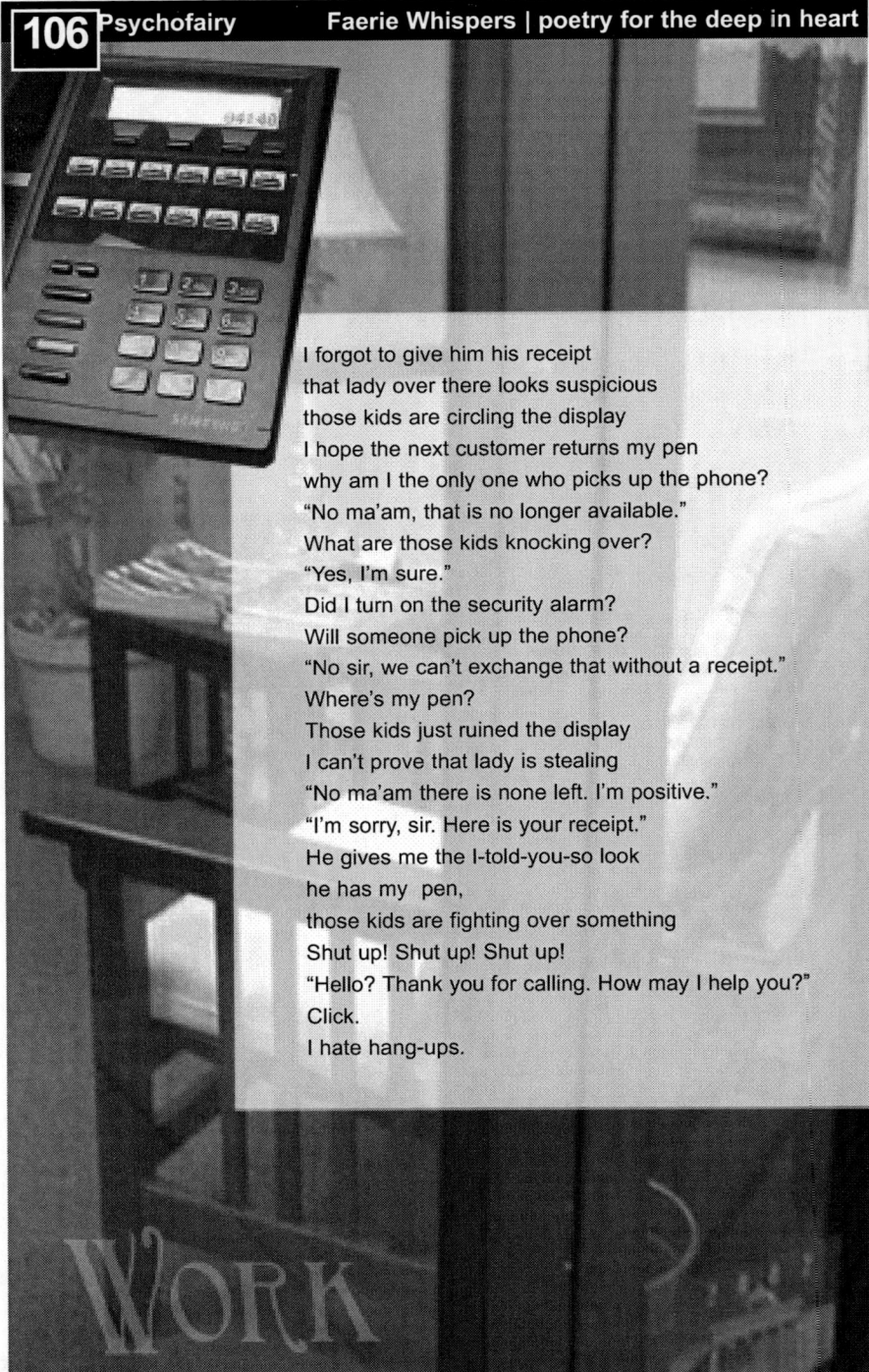

Psychofairy

Faerie Whispers | poetry for the deep in heart

I forgot to give him his receipt
that lady over there looks suspicious
those kids are circling the display
I hope the next customer returns my pen
why am I the only one who picks up the phone?
"No ma'am, that is no longer available."
What are those kids knocking over?
"Yes, I'm sure."
Did I turn on the security alarm?
Will someone pick up the phone?
"No sir, we can't exchange that without a receipt."
Where's my pen?
Those kids just ruined the display
I can't prove that lady is stealing
"No ma'am there is none left. I'm positive."
"I'm sorry, sir. Here is your receipt."
He gives me the I-told-you-so look
he has my pen,
those kids are fighting over something
Shut up! Shut up! Shut up!
"Hello? Thank you for calling. How may I help you?"
Click.
I hate hang-ups.

Psychofairy   Faerie Whispers | poetry for the deep in heart   **107**

Breaking Chains

I never thought a stranger
could be almost family
in just one week...
each day that passes
he becomes closer
more open
like a photo album on a table.
His eyes become inviting
his arms more reassuring.
I miss him when we're apart
separated by thirty miles
of terrain and traffic
only to be comforted with kisses
at the end of the day
to know we have bonded

108 Psychofairy   Faerie Whispers | poetry for the deep in heart

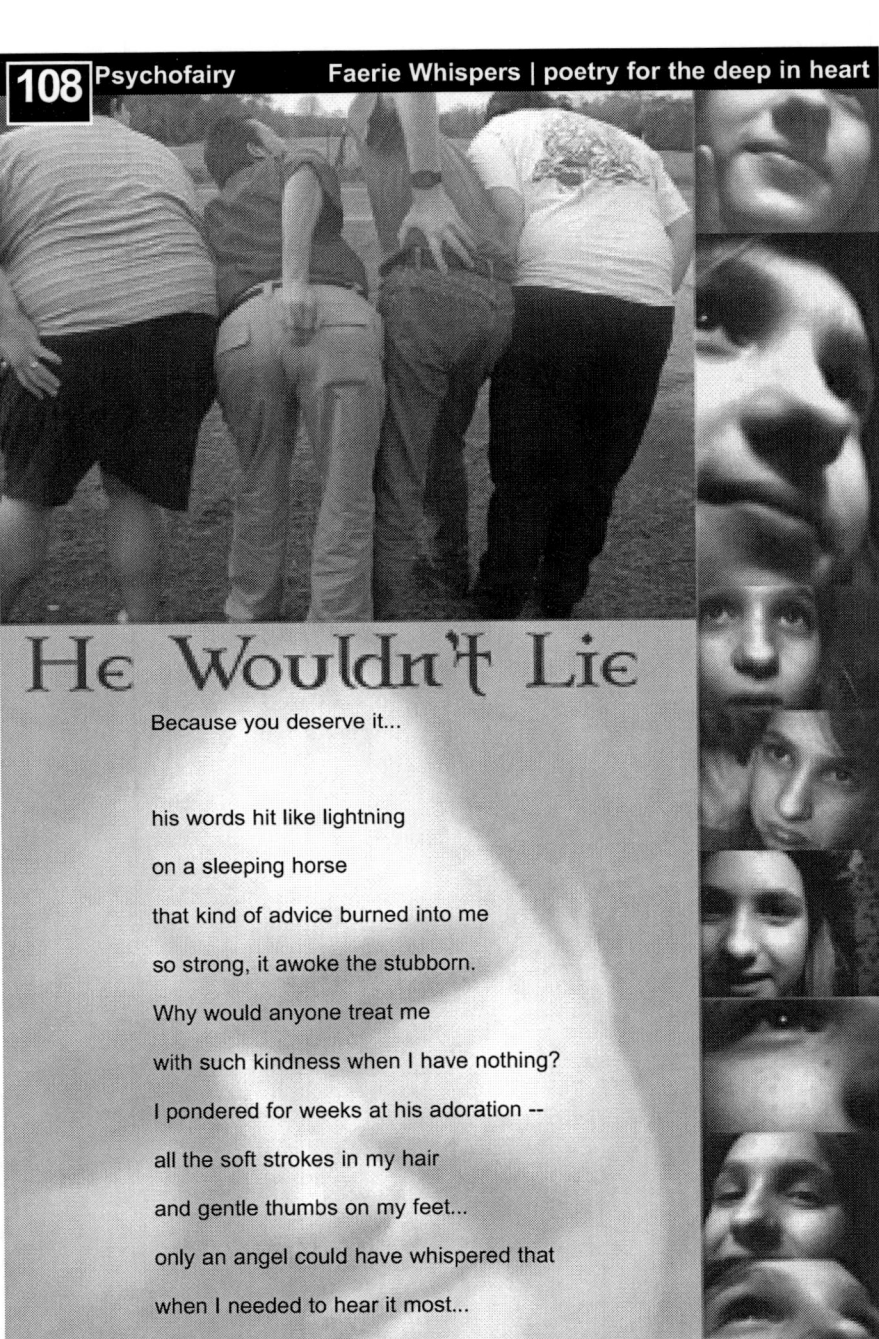

He Wouldn't Lie

Because you deserve it...

his words hit like lightning

on a sleeping horse

that kind of advice burned into me

so strong, it awoke the stubborn.

Why would anyone treat me

with such kindness when I have nothing?

I pondered for weeks at his adoration --

all the soft strokes in my hair

and gentle thumbs on my feet...

only an angel could have whispered that

when I needed to hear it most...

only a gentleman

would make me believe it.

Swimming in Sensitive Eyes

When people say eyes

are tunnels to the soul,

I knew this one was gently.

His meekness whispered

a sea of comfort

and a lake of protection

that I gladly would have swam.

The only coaxing I needed

was a sealing kiss

and I got that with a compliment.

When I fall in his eyes now,

I know heaven has allowed

one more soul,

because his eyes

have captured God too.

Psychofairy — Faerie Whispers | poetry for the deep in heart

Rant

Weary from the eight-hour drive where I had

laid my head on top of bumpy

duffel bags, legs on cup holders

now I sit in the hotel room

with my in-laws in the bed beside me,

the pool outside closed for the night,

vomit on stairs lingers

through the hallway -

tomorrow I suppose a maid will clean it

tomorrow we go to our chalet

tomorrow I will get a tattoo

maybe even write my husband's name

inside of fairy wings

let the words forever brand my butt

I'm sleepy now and the tv is loud

I will doze any second

I'm done with my cigarette

I need a new lighter

I hope I didn't leave anything in the van

I will snuggle up to my sweety

and try to fuck him while his parents sleep.

Psychofairy   Faerie Whispers | poetry for the deep in heart   111

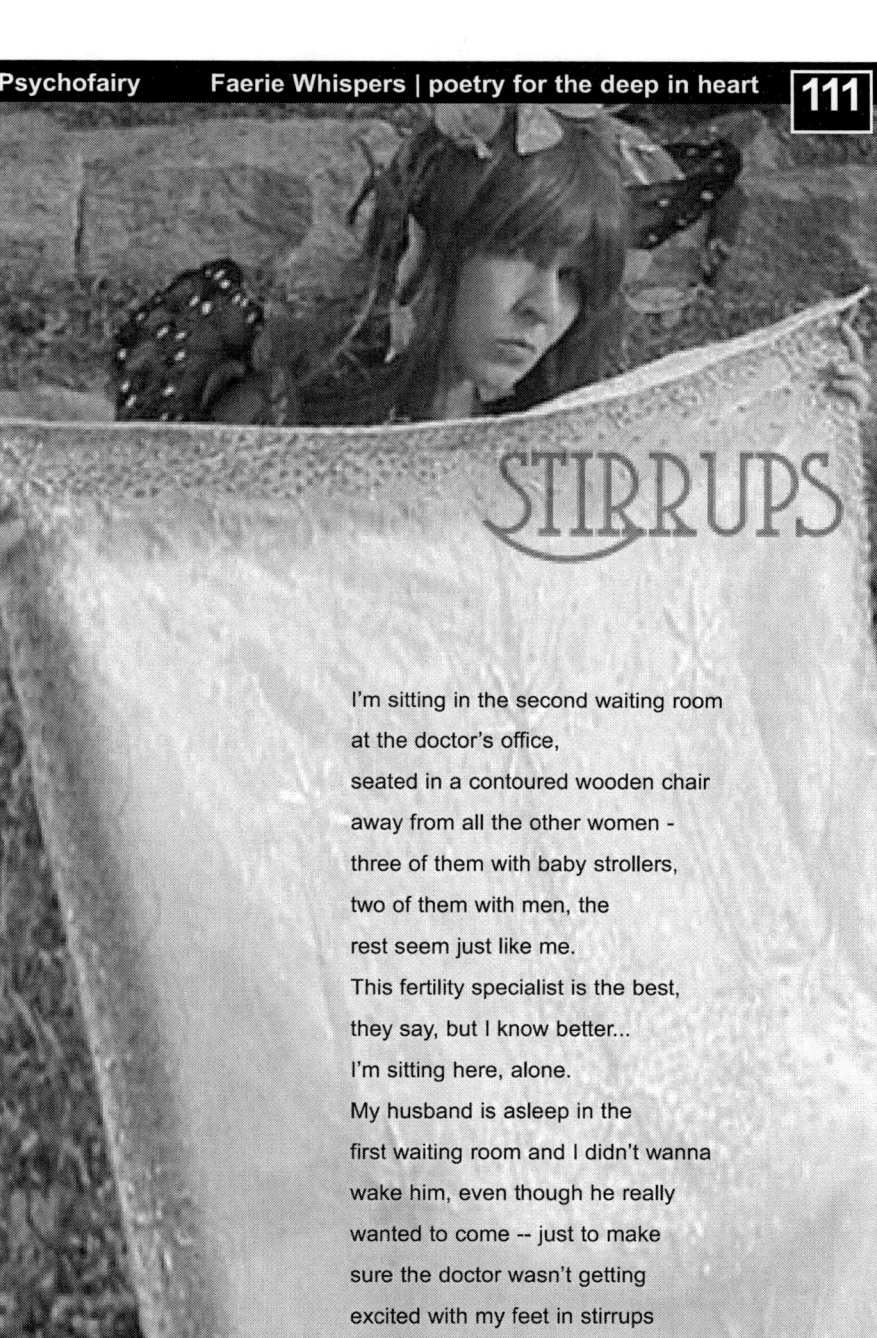

STIRRUPS

I'm sitting in the second waiting room
at the doctor's office,
seated in a contoured wooden chair
away from all the other women -
three of them with baby strollers,
two of them with men, the
rest seem just like me.
This fertility specialist is the best,
they say, but I know better...
I'm sitting here, alone.
My husband is asleep in the
first waiting room and I didn't wanna
wake him, even though he really
wanted to come -- just to make
sure the doctor wasn't getting
excited with my feet in stirrups

Psychofairy

Faerie Whispers | poetry for the deep in heart

THE LOST SOUL

In every lounge, you will find this man: brown, unclean hair. Unshaven, scruffy face. A huge beer belly with a shirt that doesn't cover his navel. An over-sized cigar close to falling out of his toothless mouth - ashes falling on his Wrangler blue jeans and cowboy boots.

He's wearing a Dodger's cap and a red, plaid long-sleeved shirt. The unbuttoned collar revealed an unattractive chest. He's shouting at the tv above the bar because his team lost. He's listening to R.E.M. while playing Poker, wearing a thick, leather belt with his name

engraved. His breast pocket is full of scraps of paper, pens, and some notes from work. His back pocket is full of Discover cards and fifty dollar bills. He's married but doesn't wear the ring. He belches at pretty waitresses in short skirts he screams for more beer when another friend arrives.

He laughs the loudest, yet becomes lonely when his friends leave his wife's got cold supper on the table she's been waiting for hours. She goes to bed. He comes in at midnight, says he was caught in traffic - again.

Psychofairy — Faerie Whispers | poetry for the deep in heart

Sometimes

(dedicated to my dad)

Sometimes we would watch
a movie just so we could
pick out mistakes and holes
sometimes we'd go out to eat
and just sit there voting
on the one person weirder than us
and crown them for it...
we would relish in their awkwardness
the fat, the skinny, the man who
scratched his dreadlocks with a
fork...
sometimes we would eat fancy
and rate the sweet tea
so we'd remember only
the South can perfect it
sometimes we'd cruise
country roads laughing
at ugly houses falling apart,
those run-down white houses
reminding us that the
president is human too
or that the ugly house
was just a step below
our run-down white shack,
one more reason to give us
the same pride as Al Bundy...
sometimes we'd belt out
annoying lyrics just to break
silence,
collect coke can tops to build
a fence around our lives...
sometimes we's make lists of or
top one hundred songs, comparing
them to see if there was
just one song we both liked
sometimes we'd sit at tables
passing paper between us,
filling in lines of poetry
to get two sets of eyes,
two sets of souls
sometimes we'd watch videos
blabber during credits
which actor played on another
movie
or dwell on that one mystery person
we never could remember
until the end
always something in life
that turns every "sometimes"
into the best dreams anyone
could ever possibly greet

Psychofairy

Faerie Whispers | poetry for the deep in heart

The Seventh sense

(for my father)

You taught me
how to relish midnight scents
of smoked wood and pine needles
and learn differently
than old men that sit in silence
with dust on their heads -
realizing their bodies will
one day become piles of manure...

We're different.
We are not lazy dogs
that don't bark -
don't just lie on our sides
and dream -
we use our voices
like shouters, treading grapes,
making the fantasies reality.

If I could tear the sky open
after you leave,
I'd ask you to paint the clouds on a canvas,
rain on leather flowers, and
build a staircase of cedar
so I could join you.

When you die,
the earth will wear out
like old moth-eaten clothing -
tombstones will bow
as blades of grass -
your words will become snow
that showers the ground
the sky will mourn with me.

But now, we still grow,
learning from our thoughts -
often floating like a deer's tail.
Petals fall every year,
and they still have their stems.
Smile daddy,
I promised to make you proud.

Psychofairy — Faerie Whispers | poetry for the deep in heart

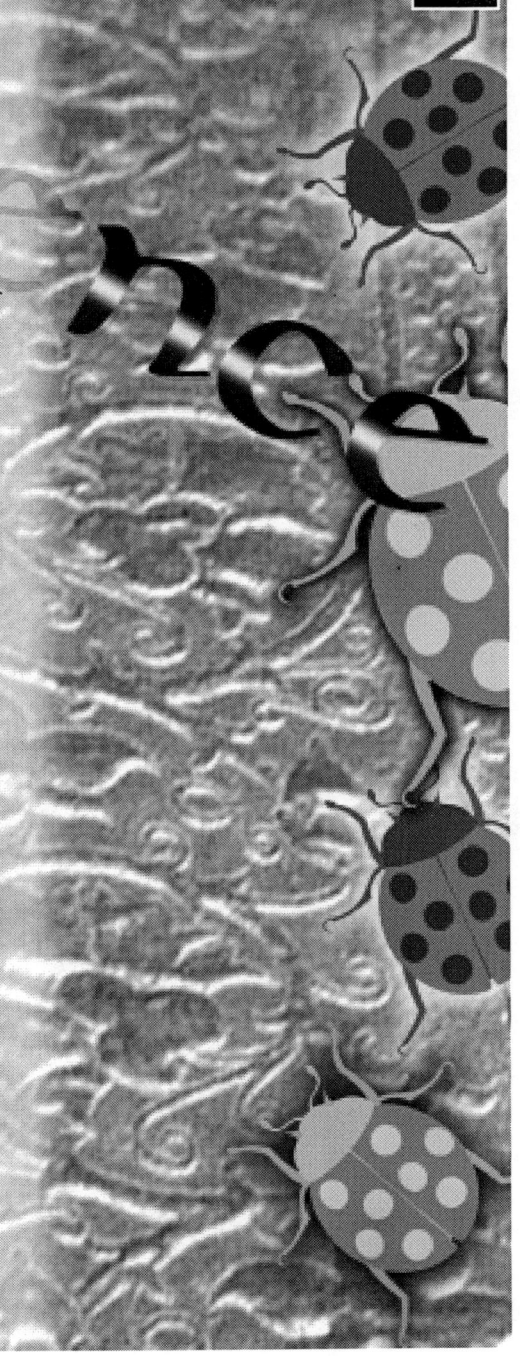

Our feet walked in circles for hours
but we never paid attention
until the leaves piled over our steps.
You spoke so softly,
I could never hear you,
but I didn't really want to -
you only muttered a few words
about grass and clouds
and all that nature stuff
I never really cared about.
You would break a branch
from a holly bush,
then tear it into tiny shreds
like you had nothing better to do
but talk about broken twigs
and how they remind you of cars.
I tried to understand you,
I tried to care,
and I even attempted to smile
but my lips only parted.
My thoughts were simple,
but you always told me what to say
like I had no voice,
no opinions about politics
and all the other things
people pretend to care about.
You never wondered what I thought
about your job and money
and even your parents,
you just assumed I agreed.
I guess I just liked
to stand beside you -
not that I wanted to,
it was just convenient.
It was easy to walk
that same trail
with nothing to say
and nothing to do,
except answer each
rhetorical question with
silence.

If you were to faint
I'd catch you
three different ways
and let my hands save you

If you were to fall
I'd try to lift you up
drag you to the sofa
or a comfortable rug

If you were to bleed
I want to be your bandage
keeping the red sealed
behind frail walls

Psychofairy   Faerie Whispers | poetry for the deep in heart

A garden of ancient mysteries
a mistaken identity of choice
and life passes slowly
while the environment
around me
envelopes a cloud
around my footsteps

The path I walk
is always open
just don't litter it, because
not everything is
easy to clean.
Be gentle with your words
my voice is softened
and beauty in life
is often misinterpreted

free your inner being
and cherish the character
you once lived

Psychofairy

Faerie Whispers | poetry for the deep in heart

Elegant Eighteen

I was seventeen last week,
couldn't vote or marry
or buy airline tickets...
but now handfuls
of junkmail crowd my box
asking me to sign up
for the Marines
or join a music club,
apply for a MasterCard,
buy life insurance,
and even Ed McMahan
says I can win $31 million.
Several very long, and
I do mean VERY long days
made me a legal adult
in most dance clubs
and strip joints.
Stores welcome me
to buy cigarettes,
lottery tickets, and tobacco.
And to make it worse,
I'm allowed to buy porn or
have an abortion.
When I read Newsweek,
I'm now in their survey
of people ages 18-29
who approves of a tax cut.
Banks open new accounts
without Mommy's signature...
but I am not any smarter,
richer or more mature
than I was seven days ago
and no one offered me money
and accounts and free services
seven days ago
and no one sat me at the adult table
seven days ago
and no one placed me on a ballot
seven days ago
so why should I spend my money
on people who only notice me
when I turn eighteen?

Psychofairy | Faerie Whispers | poetry for the deep in heart

Black Hole

I got my eyes dilated

but the world still looks clear

at 8 pm when

traffic lights seem

to stay in sync

and cop cars

stay parked behind trees

beside the cable company...

a brand new pair of

Christian Dior eyeglasses

rest comfortably on my nose

and still the glare, blur

and brightness of the moon

shade me into my own

comfort as I sit

in a passenger seat,

head tilted back

listening to an older Joan Baez

on a cheap CD player

expecting the world to fade

into a giant blurry hole

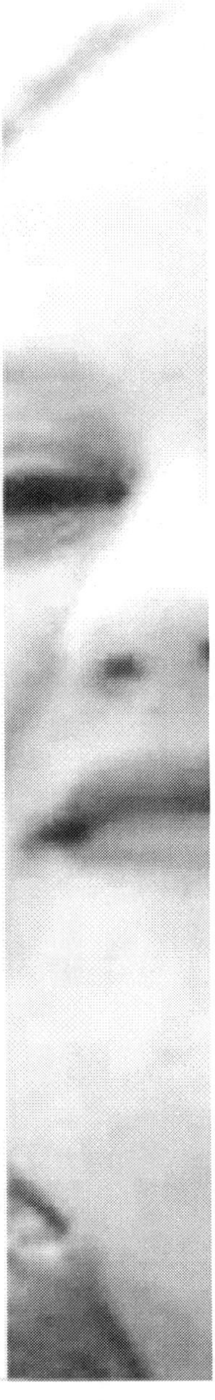

Worn Out from serving

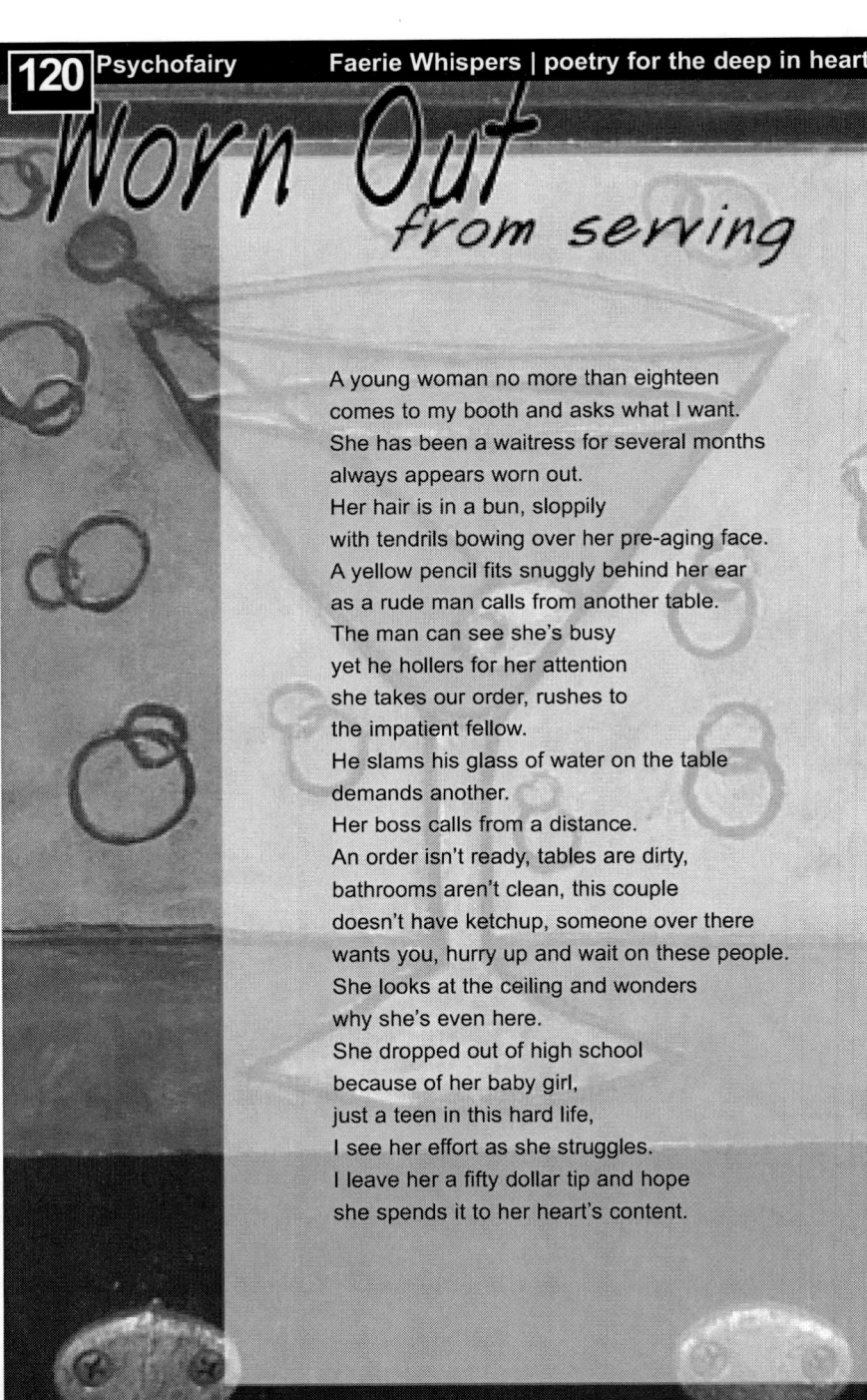

A young woman no more than eighteen
comes to my booth and asks what I want.
She has been a waitress for several months
always appears worn out.
Her hair is in a bun, sloppily
with tendrils bowing over her pre-aging face.
A yellow pencil fits snuggly behind her ear
as a rude man calls from another table.
The man can see she's busy
yet he hollers for her attention
she takes our order, rushes to
the impatient fellow.
He slams his glass of water on the table
demands another.
Her boss calls from a distance.
An order isn't ready, tables are dirty,
bathrooms aren't clean, this couple
doesn't have ketchup, someone over there
wants you, hurry up and wait on these people.
She looks at the ceiling and wonders
why she's even here.
She dropped out of high school
because of her baby girl,
just a teen in this hard life,
I see her effort as she struggles.
I leave her a fifty dollar tip and hope
she spends it to her heart's content.

Psychofairy — Faerie Whispers | poetry for the deep in heart

Adoration

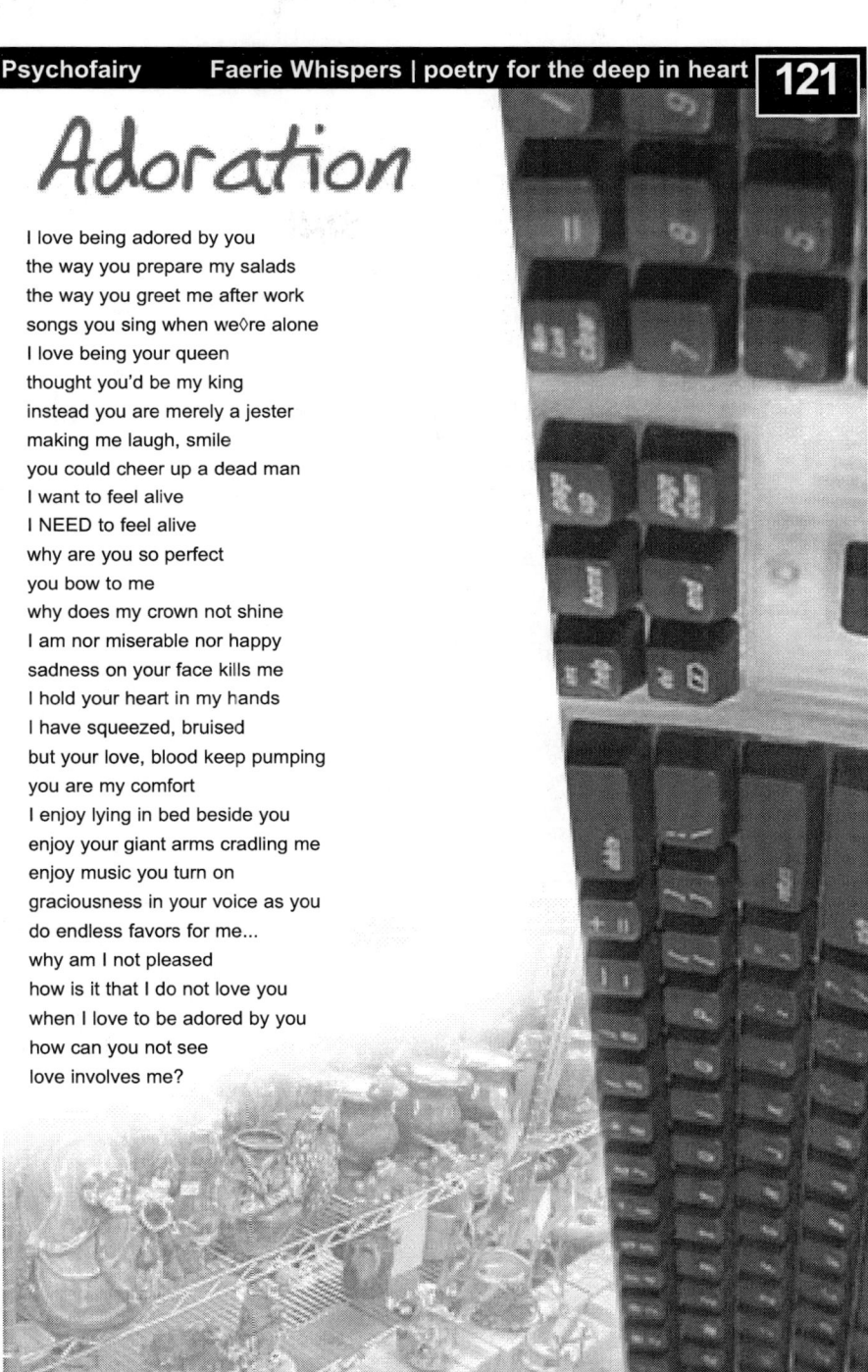

I love being adored by you
the way you prepare my salads
the way you greet me after work
songs you sing when we♢re alone
I love being your queen
thought you'd be my king
instead you are merely a jester
making me laugh, smile
you could cheer up a dead man
I want to feel alive
I NEED to feel alive
why are you so perfect
you bow to me
why does my crown not shine
I am nor miserable nor happy
sadness on your face kills me
I hold your heart in my hands
I have squeezed, bruised
but your love, blood keep pumping
you are my comfort
I enjoy lying in bed beside you
enjoy your giant arms cradling me
enjoy music you turn on
graciousness in your voice as you
do endless favors for me...
why am I not pleased
how is it that I do not love you
when I love to be adored by you
how can you not see
love involves me?

The Noble Chessmaster

he leans here gazing at my rook and his pawn,
six other people around him waiting for his move
so he could finish THEIR games,
amazing how he could play seven people at once
and no one has beaten him in days...
his homemade knight vest with a crest in the center
makes him look noble, like the rest here at the renaissance fair.
he's been thinking for minutes, which is rare,
he moves his queen to intimidate
as though he's fumbled through war to bring out peace
but he knows I'm not them,
I will not back down and I will certainly not retreat
he rotates around his circle, making his swift moves
then he comes back to our game
and realizes that this match won't be quick like the others
I could pin him in two moves
and he knows it,
I see where he could get me in one...
he gets there first. I lose.
Today, I have become his toughest match
out of forty-something people so far.
My eyes yield to the ever-growing trophy
mounted to the side of his booth

I want that trophy, I will have that trophy
it is earned by anyone who offers him the best played game
by the end of the day after everyone deserves a shot,
whether they win or lose (they always lose)...
but after four more hours of matches with more people,
he lifts that tall gold trophy above the crowd of shouting chesters
and thrusts it towards me, the woman.
"She was always one step away from checkmate the whole game,
she castled, she forked, she played hard," he chanted...
the ONLY woman in 2 years to win that coveted trophy....
I could not move. Not only have I never won a trophy,
but I rarely ever win anything. I thanked him, shook his hand
told him to start practicing, because next year, I'd come
with an armful of cash, saying I'd beat his ass
He said..."looking forward to the challenge!"
yeah, I smiled, he'll see....

Psychofairy — Faerie Whispers | poetry for the deep in heart

Soothing Tongue

my shirt's on backwards, my hair's a mess
my dog goes walking out
at 2 am I got half my pj's on
gotta put on my shoes, my husband's
sleeping restfully with his feet off the bed,
he's left the tv on and it's gradually
dying - but my baby's on his back,
and he leans over to tell me to
be right back and I kiss him quickly
and go outside...

when I return, gotta shut off the tube,
gotta slip off the shoes, gotta fluff
my pillow and steal back my sheets
I put my arm on your back, it feels so
smooth, and in return I feel your
stomach on mine and it's warm as toast
God I'd do anything to hold you this close
been meaning to sleep with you
but not really sleep with you
but not really sleep
are you awake, darling
or are you snoring?

Psychofairy
Faerie Whispers | poetry for the deep in heart

If I could be invisible
for just one night
I'd watch you
probably watch my boss and
neighbors too
I've always wondered what you
do after eight
whatcha do when your body aches
do you sit by the phone like I do
do you toss and turn like
tires like I do?

I am everywhere you are
and I'd like to think the same
about you - do you think
I'm worth watching when I'm alone?

are you watching television now
ain't it funny that your hands
speak louder than words -
what your fingers do beneath
sheets when you're watching the tube
let me know I'm on your mind

let me be everywhere with you.

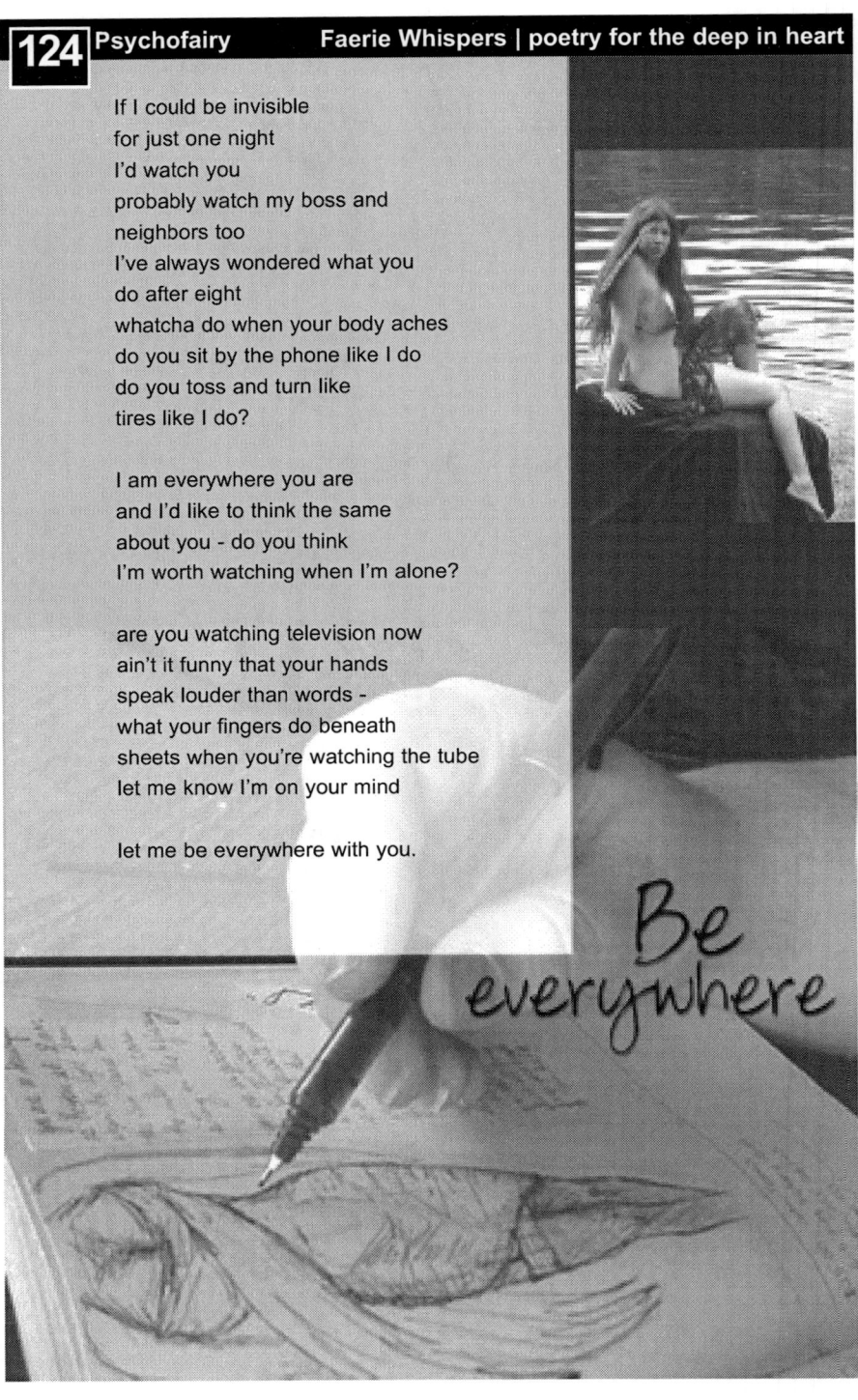

Be everywhere

Psychofairy — Faerie Whispers | poetry for the deep in heart

I felt awkward, but he sure didn't.
He sat there... eyes fixed on the television
never blinking or swallowing.
The woman took her clothes off
and I looked down.
He took his pistol from his drawer,
rested it on his lap,
and told me he'd never shot a woman,
but there was a first time for everything.
I knew he watched porno films religiously,
but never thought he'd force me to,
until last night after
masturbating to the screams of orgasms
made me perform lover's lust.
He would roll his head back
as if he were in the film
and I would hold back vomit
while he held back drool.

Affair's

The scent of last night
hasn't left the room.
Neighbor's smell it,
inching their nostrils in my direction.
How was I to know he had a wife,
the woman he was supposed to cherish?
He told me he loved me,
but I knew he loved me,
but I knew it was too soon.
Our voices were heard through walls
of his soundproof apartment,
but we couldn't help it.
He used me while his wife was away,
yet all eyes peer through blinds
as if I'm the culprit
while I walk down steps
with frizzy hair and morning breath.

Other Side

Psychofairy — Faerie Whispers | poetry for the deep in heart

I pretend to listen while you tell me how
well your boy is doing in school
I nod and smile and laugh
but deep down I am thinking of all the ways
I hate you -
for being so lucky
for having a family
for having more than one life
I am a victim
and punishing myself, the books say
as though I am just a statistic
amongst the infertile.
I am childless
I have to repeat that
I am childless
how come it took me five minutes to say that?
childless
child...less
why does it hurt so much to say that?
it used to never hurt before
why do parents joke about lending out their kids -
how cruel
why do parents say to stop trying so hard -
oh save it, stress is not the cause, it is the outcome
why do parents say this is meant to be -
yeah let's see them say that if they walked were me.
you're not childless
childless
parents, imagine life without your kids
puts things in perspective doesn't it?

Psychofairy

Faerie Whispers | poetry for the deep in heart

walking through the door
as I came home that Tuesday night
everything around me seemed to
follow me to the bathroom
the walls stared at me
as though they wish they could help
but not like those pair of eyes
I saw an hour ago peering behind
that red Mazda in the parking lot.
he could have called the police
he could have honked his horn
he could have just turned on the car
he could have yelled
he could have helped
he could have...
but while I was being butchered
by this man I wish I never met
I had to lay there knowing
someone was watching,
which was crueler than the act itself.
I stepped into the shower
and the glass door seemed to have
eyes peering through as well...
the eyes.
the eyes.
following me everywhere.

Bad Samaritan

Psychofairy

Faerie Whispers | poetry for the deep in heart

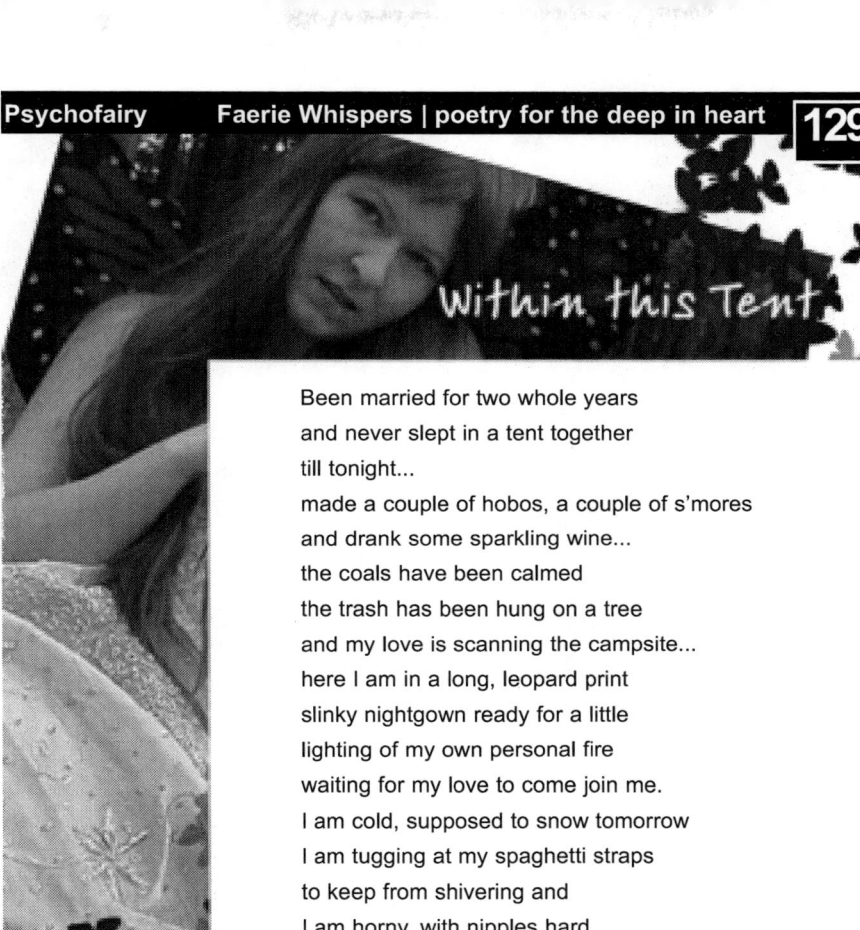

Within this Tent

Been married for two whole years
and never slept in a tent together
till tonight...
made a couple of hobos, a couple of s'mores
and drank some sparkling wine...
the coals have been calmed
the trash has been hung on a tree
and my love is scanning the campsite...
here I am in a long, leopard print
slinky nightgown ready for a little
lighting of my own personal fire
waiting for my love to come join me.
I am cold, supposed to snow tomorrow
I am tugging at my spaghetti straps
to keep from shivering and
I am horny, with nipples hard
and my mouth throbbing for warmth...
my hands crave affection within
this tiny tent made for two -
no tv, no radio, no telephone, not even a watch...
just the two of us dependent on skin
to fill the appetite we crave.
It's our anniversary weekend that makes
us travel to go play, like children at camp,
but this time, there's no parents to guide us
or tell us to behave and keep our hands apart...
we have become adults
whose desire never fades
and whose hands never separate....

Psychofairy

Faerie Whispers | poetry for the deep in heart

when you come alone
I can hold your hand
and when your heart is here
I'll let you know it's for real
but where do you stand
when others take the blame
and you lean there on my door

when you see the light
I'll let you feel my soul
and when you smell the breeze
I'll let you take control
but you gotta know
there's two in this world
that the light that shines
grows brighter by the day

when you let me in
when you help me in
when you give in to everything
I won't hold back
I won't hold back

When you see the view
of all the mountains
and the creeks that flow from here
you'll take me there
and hold me there
and tell me it's okay

body music

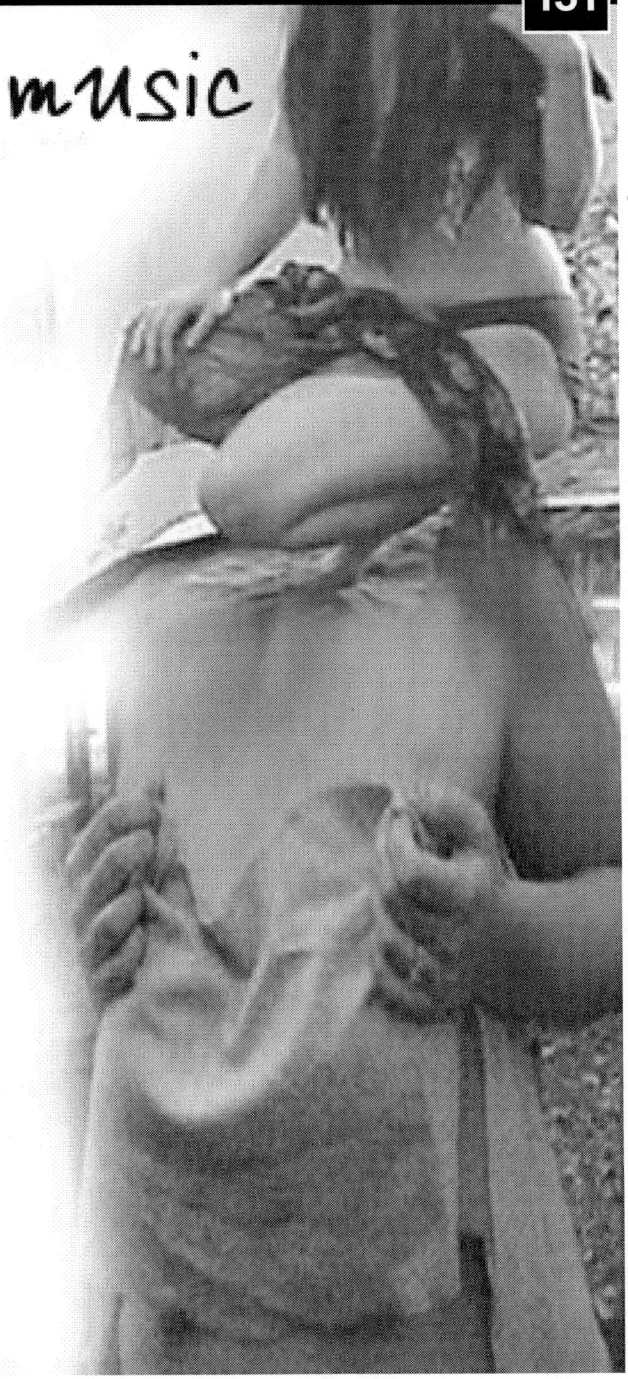

can you feel that?
that hard thump
beneath your palm
that's my heart
wanting you.
hold me...
just let me spoon
with you.
my body
screams ecstacy
and I just wanna take
you away
let the night dance
as we
create our own
body music

you

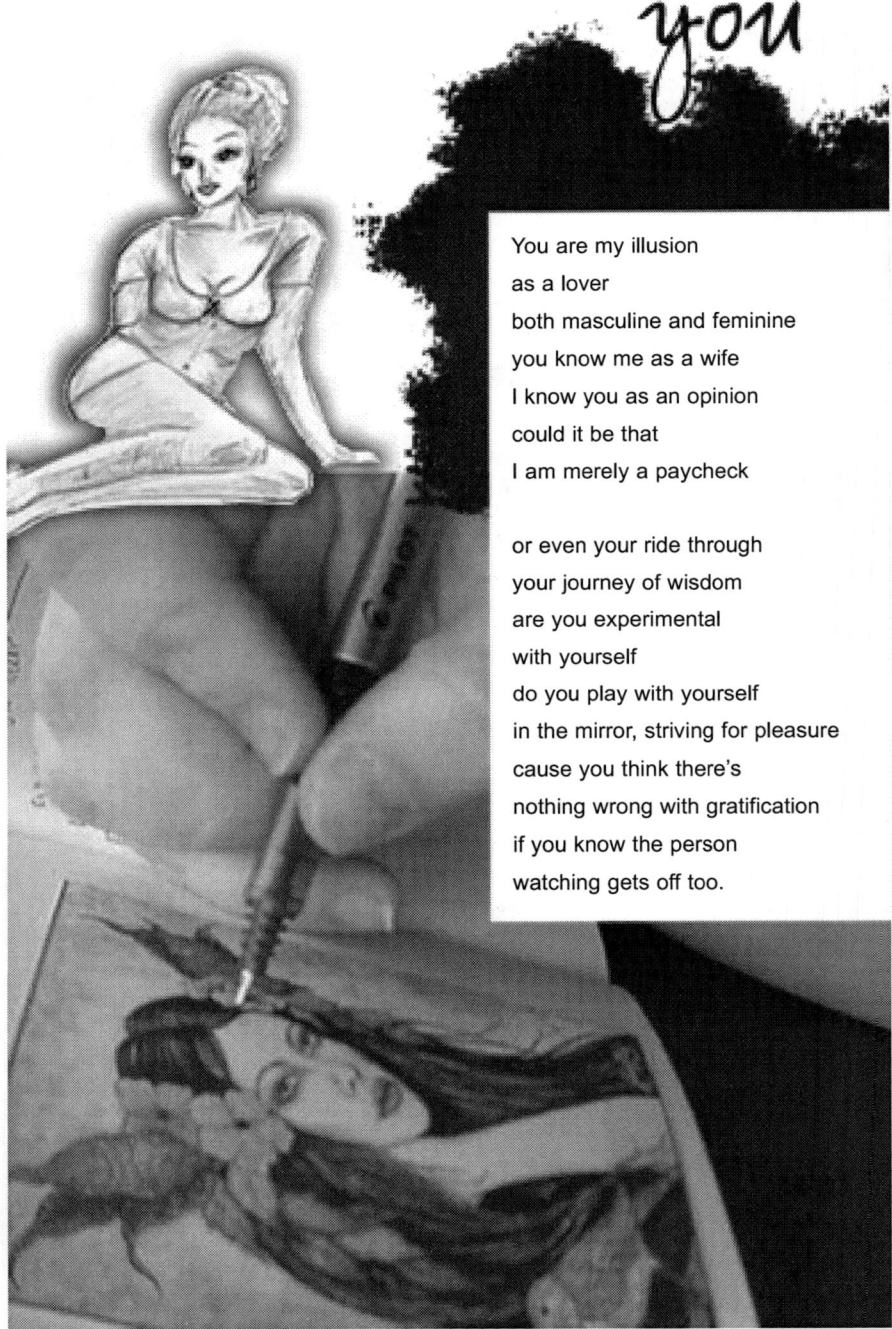

You are my illusion
as a lover
both masculine and feminine
you know me as a wife
I know you as an opinion
could it be that
I am merely a paycheck

or even your ride through
your journey of wisdom
are you experimental
with yourself
do you play with yourself
in the mirror, striving for pleasure
cause you think there's
nothing wrong with gratification
if you know the person
watching gets off too.

Psychofairy
Faerie Whispers | poetry for the deep in heart

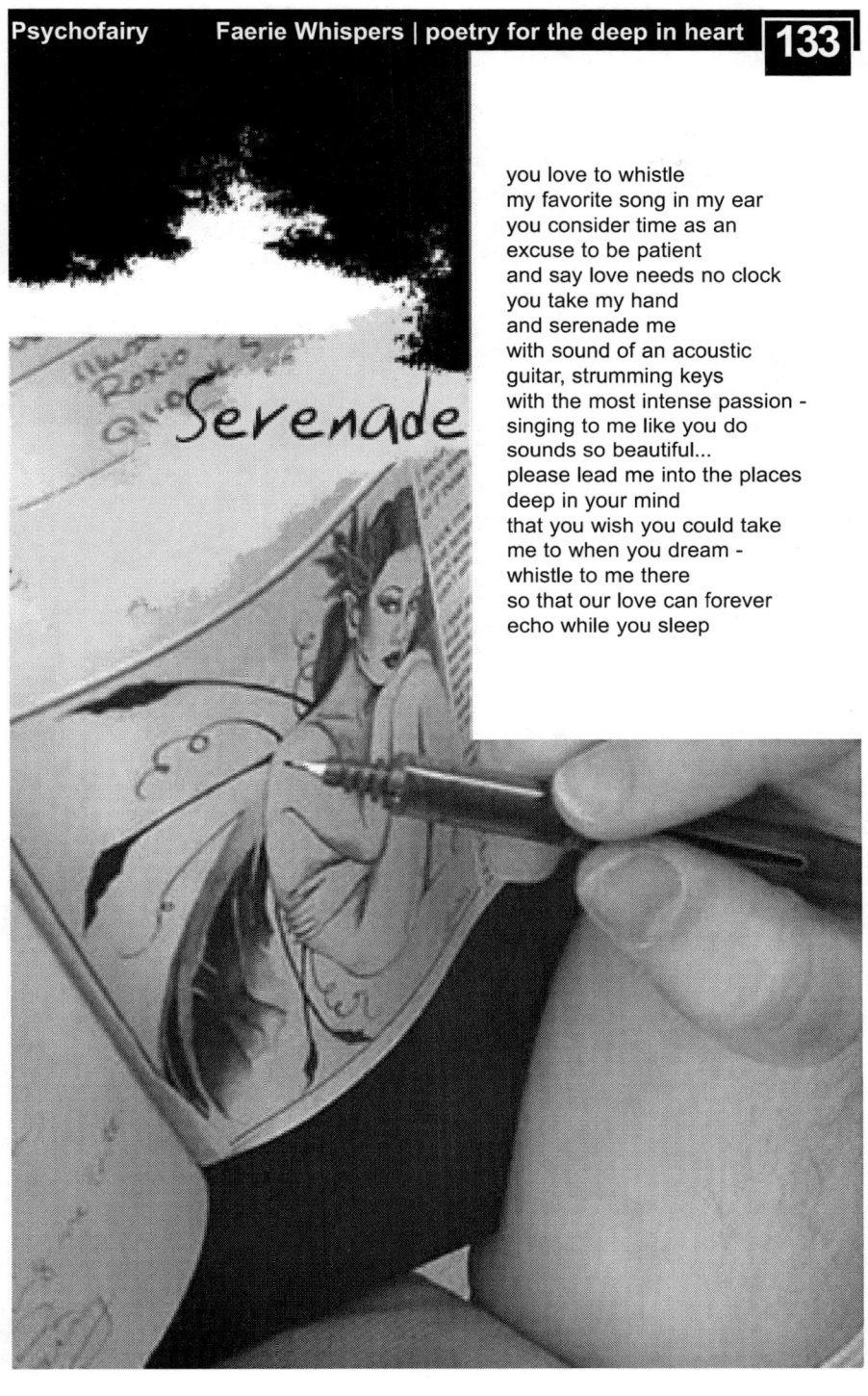

Serenade

you love to whistle
my favorite song in my ear
you consider time as an
excuse to be patient
and say love needs no clock
you take my hand
and serenade me
with sound of an acoustic
guitar, strumming keys
with the most intense passion -
singing to me like you do
sounds so beautiful...
please lead me into the places
deep in your mind
that you wish you could take
me to when you dream -
whistle to me there
so that our love can forever
echo while you sleep

Psychofairy — Faerie Whispers | poetry for the deep in heart

Timeline

I've been alone,
so alone that my car was my only solace,
been dependent on people
so dependent I relied on them for food and beds
been bruised, tied, touched
by strangers wanting to show me their power
been single and flirtatious,
so all guys would fall in my girlish trap
been dumped by handsome men,
used to cry myself to sleep thinking it was me
been married to perfection
had to wake up feeling I was unworthy
been broker than bankruptcy
with credit people nagging my answering machine
been handed high-paying jobs
and had them stripped by fraudulent bosses
been hired at minimum wage
had to work my way bagging groceries
been foolish
so foolish, I would befriend criminals for mutual affection
been young,
so young that I knew I was right
been honest with myself,
been old,
so old I felt ancient leaving the office
so honest I taught myself the truth
learned how to grow, and just be...
been beautiful
so beautiful even I thought so
been alive
so alive I loved to live
now it's not been...
just being

Psychofairy — Faerie Whispers | poetry for the deep in heart

Can't even stay safe in my
own room without someone
giving me their praise for
their newly conceived pregnancies

whether by phone, mail or
glancing through a magazine -
either in my friend or
a closely admired celebrity is
now a baby-carrying robot

or maybe I'm the robot
cause I've lost any genuine emotions
of baby praise for new mommies
could care less about baby showers
or shopping for someone else's
baby strollers and pacifiers

I'm past the sadness stage
I'm past the anger stage
for once, I feel nothing
my heart, numbed by infertility

Numbed

Rejected

Another rejection from
just another handsome man
what's so wrong with being
fat or frumpy when my
heart's in the right place?
I know lots about life,
loss and growth
and you make me feel
so unsexy when I walk by,
can't you see my smile the way I do?
Even I think I'm beautiful,
got great tits and
lovely hips, large
may they be,
I've got
conversation that never
disappears, an opinion that
will captivate you for years,
if you'd just pay a little
attention and stop tossing
me to the floor like
some chew toy, maybe
I may sit beside you

Psychofairy — Faerie Whispers | poetry for the deep in heart

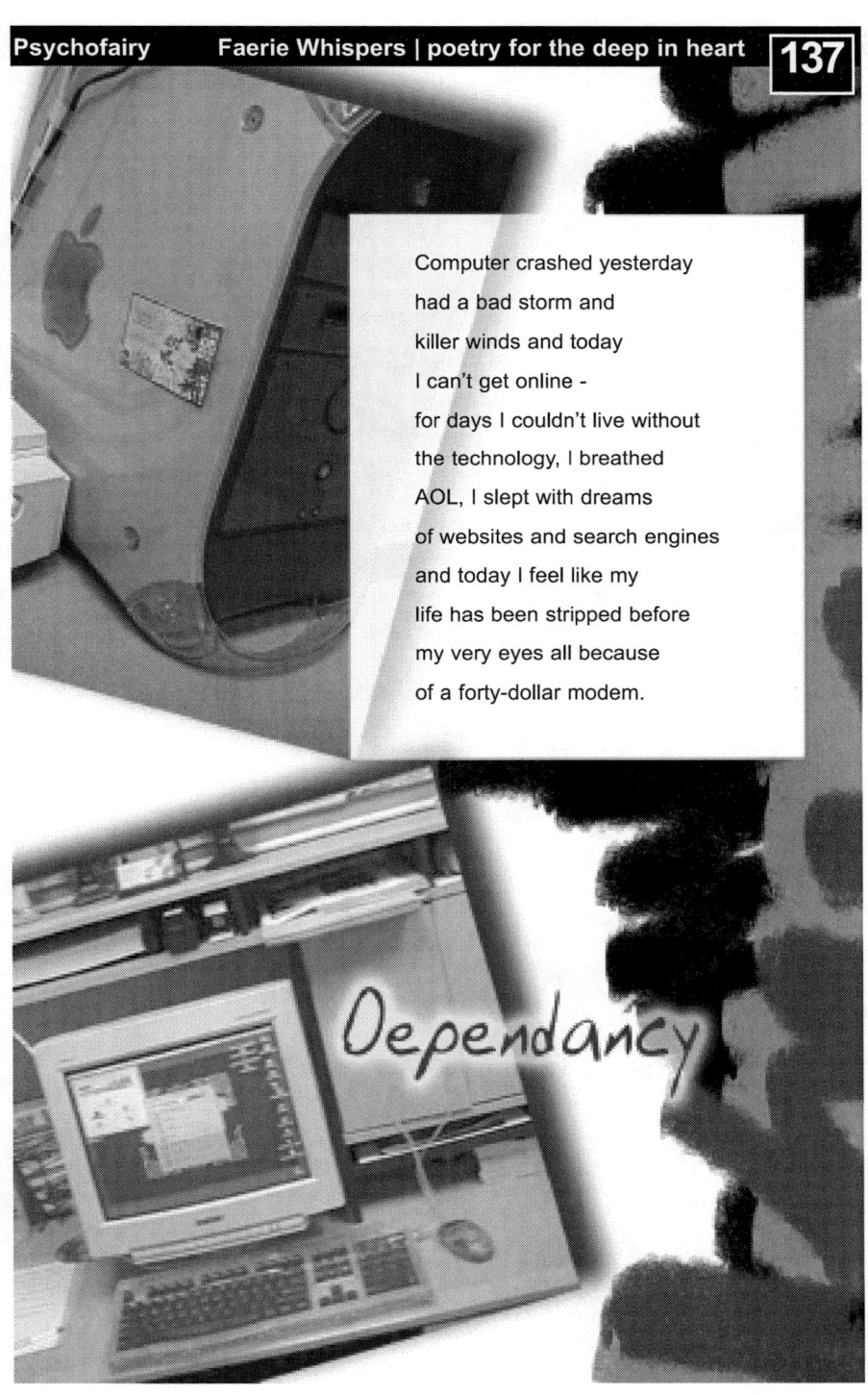

Computer crashed yesterday
had a bad storm and
killer winds and today
I can't get online -
for days I couldn't live without
the technology, I breathed
AOL, I slept with dreams
of websites and search engines
and today I feel like my
life has been stripped before
my very eyes all because
of a forty-dollar modem.

Dependancy

138 Psychofairy · Faerie Whispers | poetry for the deep in heart

TIRED OF

Tired of Huggies commercials
with some cute baby walking
to the bathroom, tired of watching
Firestone ads with some
bubbly boy sitting inside a tire,
tired of going to restaurants with
kid menus printed on the back,
waiting in line behind a school bus
watching kids running to their
front doors to greet parents,
tired of hearing news of
pregnancies from all of my
friends, coworkers and all
my husband's family, tired
of waiting behind children
at the movie theater who want
to see a Disney film, tired of
every single cotton-pickin'
person being pregnant, even my dog,
tired of going to scrapbook
parties where all the ladies talk
about their sons and their softball
practices, tired of going to Wal-Mart
and walking past the toy section,
tired of seeing babies everywhere,
even on packages of toilet paper,
on postcards, on Tylenol, on
grocery bags, even on a sticker on
my mattress, tired of not being
able to escape non-motherhood,
tired of seeing children at
upholstery shops and video stores,
tired of passing the children's section at every
single book store, tired of seeing baby shoes
at shoe stores, tired of feeling
left out of the loop, tired of being
the different one, tired of being tired.

Psychofairy   Faerie Whispers | poetry for the deep in heart

Sometimes I wish I had money like Celine Dion
where with just a hundred grand,
I could pay off my three credit cards,
finish car payments and insurance notes...
would like a new kitchen with glass cabinets
and a rotating pantry and even a marble island -
have granite countertops and the best knives...
would like to replace all the brown carpet
with dark green berber carpet
and fix all the limp, non-locking doors -
would like a porch deck with two sets
of spiral stairs surrounded by a garden -
would like a bench swing where I can
watch the sunset after work...
would like to buy a piano and learn how to play -
like to build a giant kidney-shaped swimming pool
and a matching jacuzzi spa...
would like to cover the ugly red brick
around the house with beautifully cut stones,
would like to buy a king-sized bed with a sensual
canopy and maybe add a fireplace to the bedroom...
would like a round, large bath with Roman steps
with beautiful pewter faucets and massage heads...
would like to throw away all the air conditioning units
and buy central air and heat to protect
from the winter cold and summer scorch -
would like to build a second floor so I can
have a balcony to overlook the lake across the street...
sometimes I wish I had the money
to replace our tattered blue sofa with
a new matching living room set -
throw away our cheap table and breaking,
mismatched chairs with wrought iron...
would like an outdoor set to place
on the porch and maybe even buy a
professional zoom telescope so I can see Saturn...
would like to start my own online business
so I can work at home so I won't have
to leave town after we settle home
with a newly bought baby, adopted from California -
anything left over would help us live,
to help us with bills and luxuries
but I am no Celine, I have no ending wallet,
and I've got forty dollars in the bank.

| 140 | Psychofairy | Faerie Whispers | poetry for the deep in heart |

got caught selling illegal stuff
online this week
selling things under the table
that shouldn't have been out
in the open for the universe to have...
I made hundreds of dollars profit
in just a few hours
and it just made my stomach
feel weak, so limp
especially when they sent me a
warning letter to stop
could've done time.
But what if I didn't get caught?
Would I become a millionaire in a month?
I find myself baffled at today's
market where people cannot
buy freely without the worry
of copyrights, trademarks, and registrations

copyright
MADNESS

Psychofairy — Faerie Whispers | poetry for the deep in heart

a turning year old

I imagine you turning a year old today
me and daddy are shopping for your new clothes
and tomorrow your picture will be taken
by a Sears professional -
you've already said two or three words
making your first step is only weeks away...
we watched the movie Mulan on video yesterday
bought the DVD just for you
maybe today I'll hum a song by Jewel or
give you the red bear you've been wanting.
I'm sorry for coming home late from work
I was stuck in traffic...really
daycare's not bad is it?
I hear they have to hold you a little longer,
Some of the other kids get jealous
when you get all the attention -
why do you always cry when daddy drops you off?
you know he visits for lunch
grandma stays for hours by your side
and rocks you gently to sleep
please excuse daddy's friends for being so loud
they didn't mean to wake you
they're playing pool in the other room
and forgot you were sleeping,
please don't be mad.
Mommy's here and I just want to hold you
just a little longer...
there will come a time in your life when
you won't want me to hug you
so I want to relish this as long as it lasts
cause there was once a time
we thought you'd never come
and now that you're here
we want to take every photo we can,
introduce you to the world we know
and teach you the marvels of life,
the wonders of friendship and
the feeling of family

Amazing

you amazed me again
you stirred our dinner I started
while I stepped into the other room
fed the pets before they barked
did laundry before I looked in the closet

you amazed me again
told your friends to leave early
so we could share time
you made the bed
turned on melancholy music
read me classic poetry

you amazed me again
said I love you for no reason
gave me a kiss when I wasn't leaving
told me I was beautiful without me asking
combed my hair with your fingers
so your hands could feel what
I was thinking

| Psychofairy | Faerie Whispers | poetry for the deep in heart | 143 |

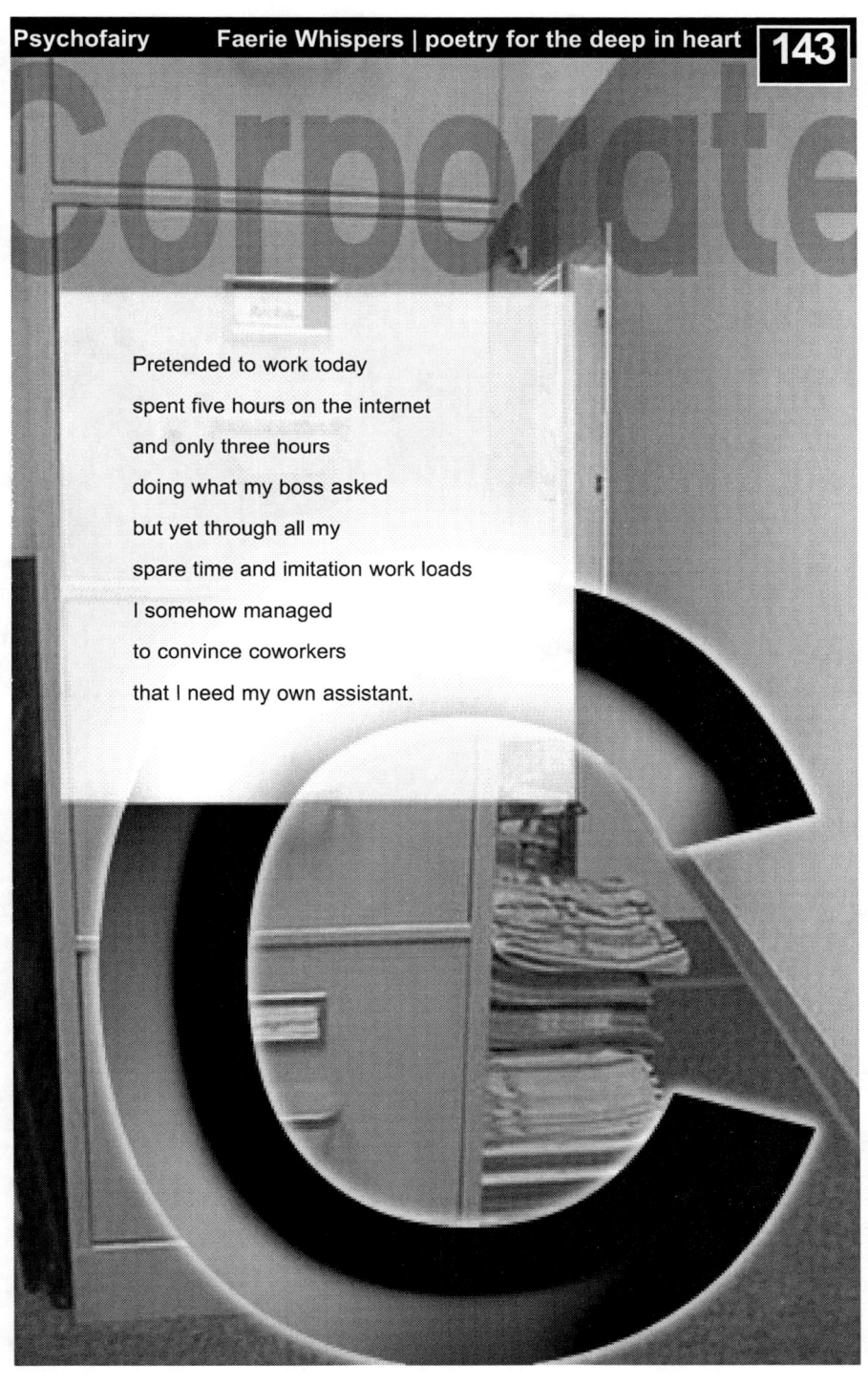

Pretended to work today

spent five hours on the internet

and only three hours

doing what my boss asked

but yet through all my

spare time and imitation work loads

I somehow managed

to convince coworkers

that I need my own assistant.

144 Psychofairy   Faerie Whispers | poetry for the deep in heart

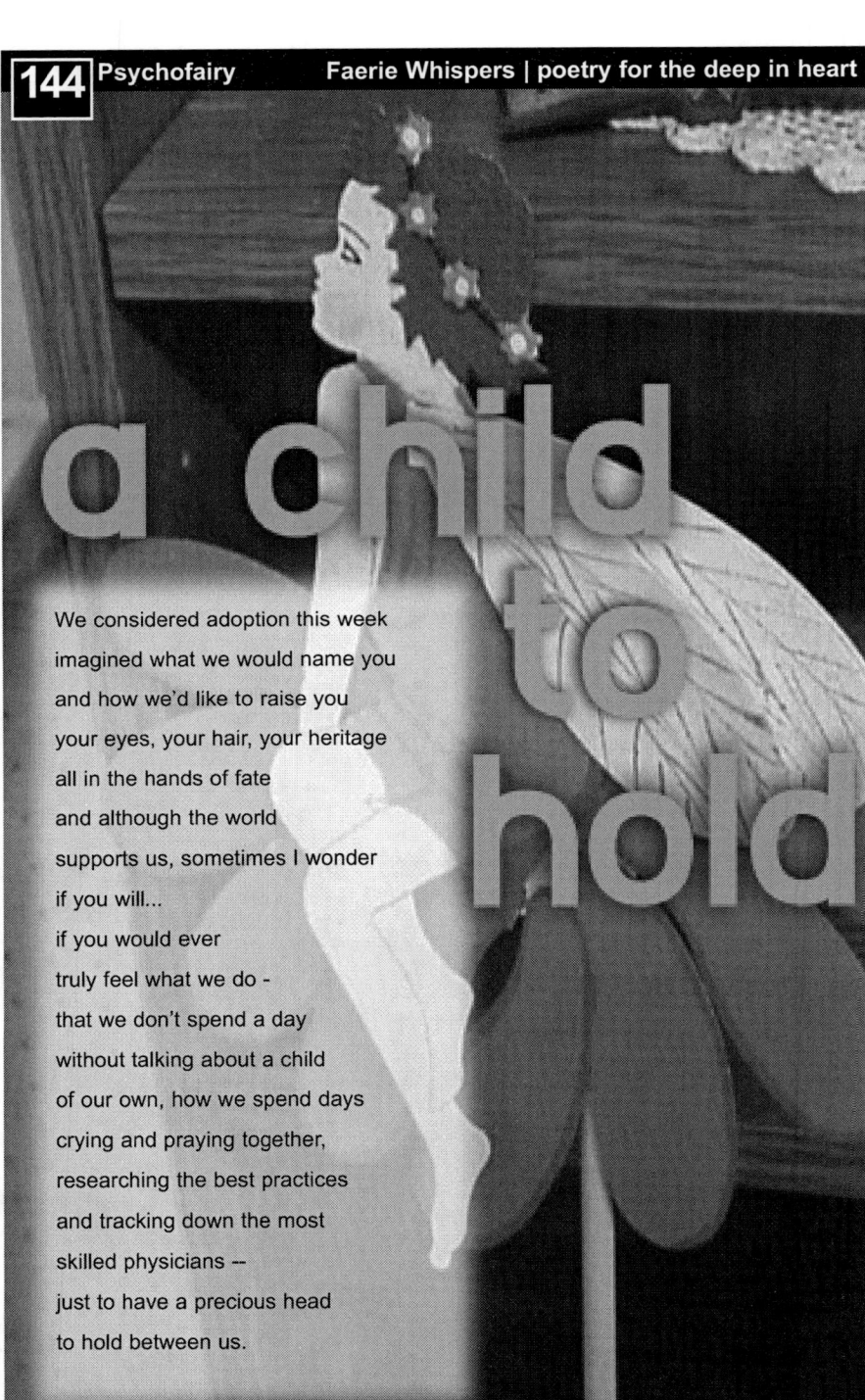

a child to hold

We considered adoption this week
imagined what we would name you
and how we'd like to raise you
your eyes, your hair, your heritage
all in the hands of fate
and although the world
supports us, sometimes I wonder
if you will...
if you would ever
truly feel what we do -
that we don't spend a day
without talking about a child
of our own, how we spend days
crying and praying together,
researching the best practices
and tracking down the most
skilled physicians --
just to have a precious head
to hold between us.

Psychofairy — Faerie Whispers | poetry for the deep in heart

Beautiful

I feel so beautiful
right now
and you haven't even
said hello...
all you have to do
is show up
so sweet and serene
and not say a
single word
and my world
falls into place..
you make me
feel so beautiful
so unbelievable
and positively
beautiful...
you capture my heart
just standing beside me -
the feeling of love
is so peaceful,
smile if you feel
that way too.

July 4th at 12:48 am

Left the movies late that night
missed the fireworks and parade
I was tired but alert,
bored but not weary,
quiet, but not restless -
driving down Redland Road
the moon was gone, the stars
were hidden and no lights
seen for miles - I saw something
I would never ever forget...
the night sky was clear
clearer than a transparent moon
no fog for miles
not a trace of white smoke
and my husband was dozing off beside me -
drove above a tall hill
and upon descent spotted two
grayish-bluish mists, more blue than gray
and one of the mists was shaped like
a person
a mysterious silhouette standing in the street
holding an item or a child...
I never caught a glimpse at the second mist
I was so afraid this could be a real person,
so I swerved to the right, jerking the car with me
as I did, one lurched at me
so much that it jolted my husband awake
and we were both too scared to speak
he turned in his seat and looked back
and saw what I saw...and we sat there
for fifteen minutes not saying a thing
but we both recorded the time,
and vowed we would visit the next year
same time, same place, same spot.

Actual Untouched Photos

Psychofairy
Faerie Whispers | poetry for the deep in heart

campground spying game

In a campground full of generator powered
RV's, we are the only fools
to pitch a tent in this cold weather.
The frigidness of the air is awkward
even to our sheltered fire and
melted marshmallows.
In every rotating glance, we see some
other family, couple, or lonesome
making their night a little more cozy.
On this anniversary trip, I just happened to
bring binoculars that enjoy the
voyeuristic habits of my prying eyes.
To my left, I spy a mother and son laying out
blankets on their camper bed.
To my right, I see a young man smoking a joint
and reading a thick book...hmmm
across a long path, I can spot a couple
making love - but my binoculars only make out
a shadowed silhouette of a woman on top of a man
my husband sees me watching and tells me
to stop cause its rude, but seems to me
like he wanted to see too, cause he was
very interested in their motions.
But I must say they gave us an inspiration
to compete with this persistently happy couple
and provide any other spying eyes
with a taste of our own public love session.

Adoption meets Reality

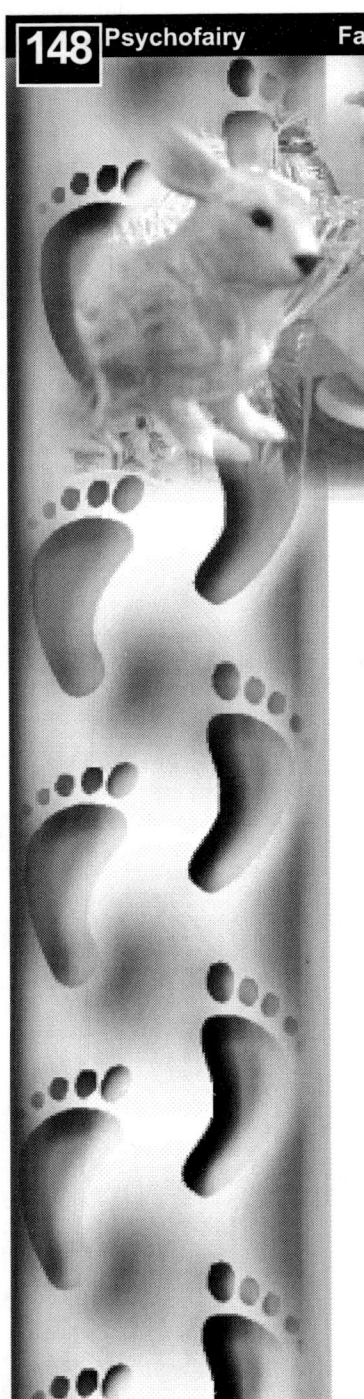

adoption...now that's a big word.
a last resort
you know, if things "didn't work out"
in the whole egg department
seems easy enough
prove to be good parents
smile for social workers
show them your large house
everything will be fine

reality. background checks.
oh dear, my husband's seizures
my medical history ugh!
credit checks. so I really don't
have that much money, and
I'm late with payments sometimes,
family history, great of course
we get along fine -
I ran away at 17 and my
family lives in separate states
and my mom and I don't speak
my sis got hitched without
telling me, of course our family is close.

I thought I could be ready
maybe I am still a child wanting
one for all the wrong reasons
maybe I just want a kid
to prove I am not my mother
maybe I am not as great as I thought
maybe I still have issues

Psychofairy
Faerie Whispers | poetry for the deep in heart

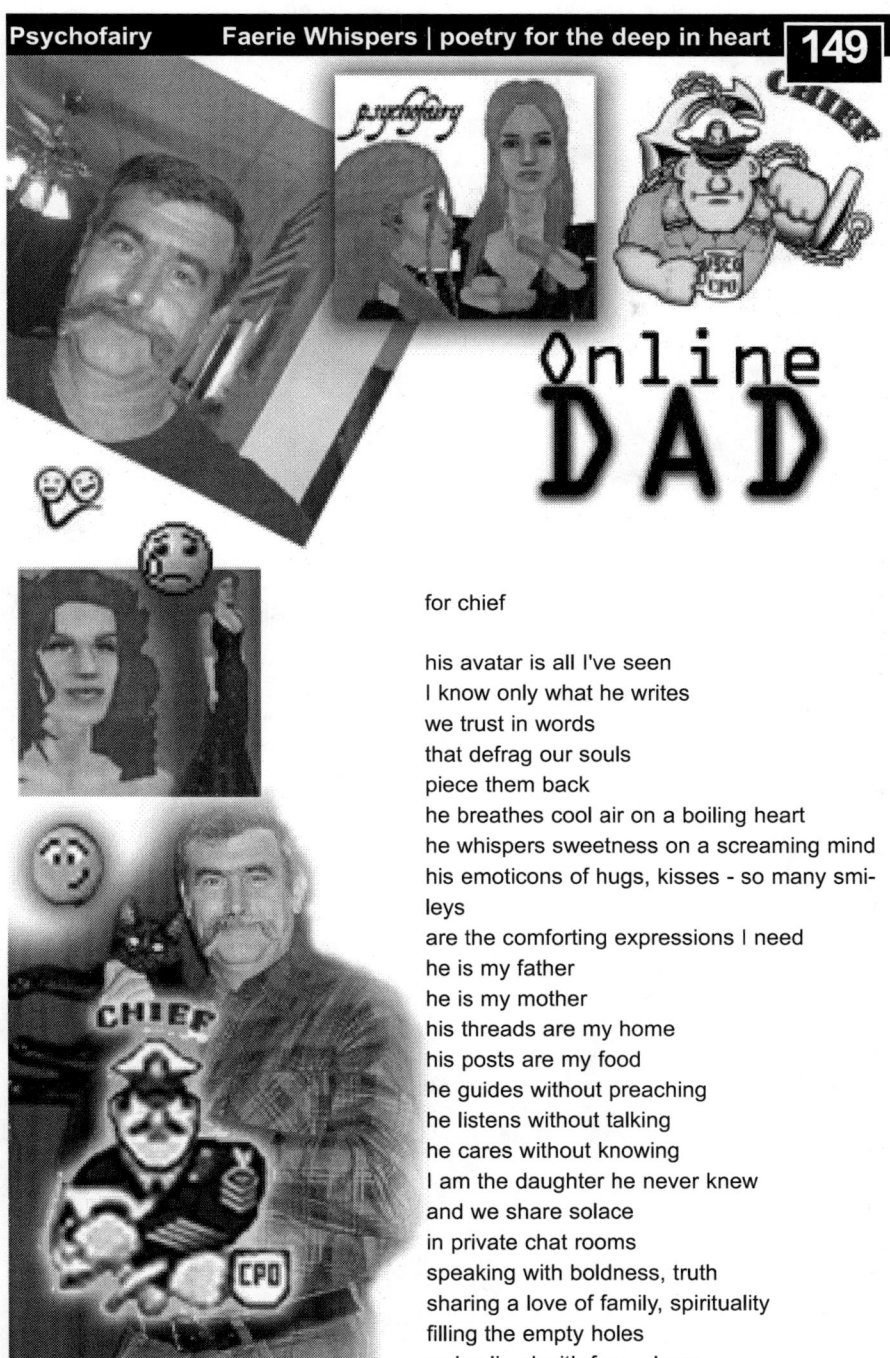

Online DAD

for chief

his avatar is all I've seen
I know only what he writes
we trust in words
that defrag our souls
piece them back
he breathes cool air on a boiling heart
he whispers sweetness on a screaming mind
his emoticons of hugs, kisses - so many smileys
are the comforting expressions I need
he is my father
he is my mother
his threads are my home
his posts are my food
he guides without preaching
he listens without talking
he cares without knowing
I am the daughter he never knew
and we share solace
in private chat rooms
speaking with boldness, truth
sharing a love of family, spirituality
filling the empty holes
we've lived with for so long...

150 Psychofairy

Faerie Whispers | poetry for the deep in heart

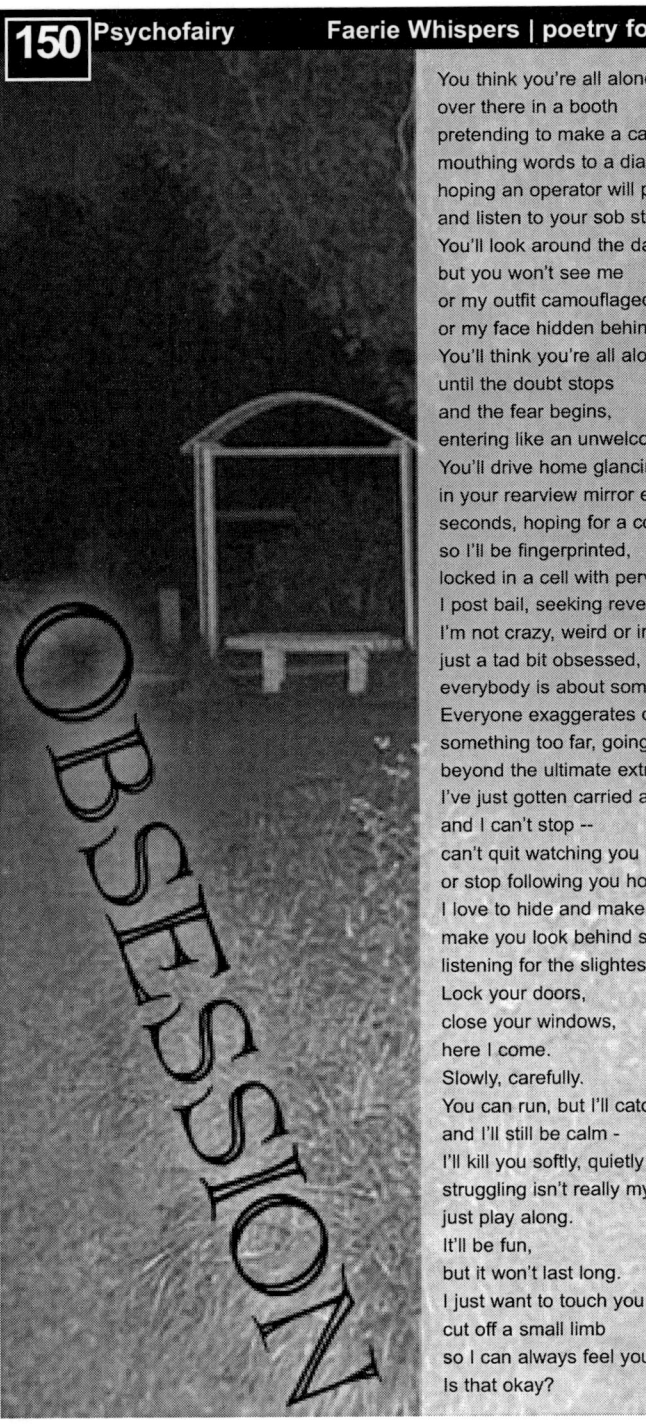

You think you're all alone
over there in a booth
pretending to make a call
mouthing words to a dial tone
hoping an operator will pick up
and listen to your sob story.
You'll look around the darkness
but you won't see me
or my outfit camouflaged by bushes
or my face hidden behind leaves.
You'll think you're all alone
until the doubt stops
and the fear begins,
entering like an unwelcome visitor.
You'll drive home glancing
in your rearview mirror every few
seconds, hoping for a cop
so I'll be fingerprinted,
locked in a cell with perverts until
I post bail, seeking revenge.
I'm not crazy, weird or insane...
just a tad bit obsessed,
everybody is about something.
Everyone exaggerates or takes
something too far, going
beyond the ultimate extreme.
I've just gotten carried away
and I can't stop --
can't quit watching you sleep
or stop following you home.
I love to hide and make you scared,
make you look behind shadows,
listening for the slightest footsteps.
Lock your doors,
close your windows,
here I come.
Slowly, carefully.
You can run, but I'll catch you
and I'll still be calm -
I'll kill you softly, quietly
struggling isn't really my thing -
just play along.
It'll be fun,
but it won't last long.
I just want to touch you
cut off a small limb
so I can always feel you.
Is that okay?

Psychofairy

Faerie Whispers | poetry for the deep in heart

careless

when I'm careless
your needs fly over my head
when I'm careless
I yell and scream
and get my way
and the look on your face
makes me wince in pain -
you look like a man
whose lost his wife,
lost any happiness or hope

it's all my fault
I knew it when I said it
and I even know it now
what triggers these
emotions to make
me hurt you like
a selfish cionide
can you forgive me
and let me start again
I'll be good
I'll be better
and tonight you will see
that passion comes from
forgiveness and it's been
a while since I've been sorry.

152 Psychofairy   Faerie Whispers | poetry for the deep in heart

I'll admit to caring too much
for selling out my soul
to a childhood dream
come true by seventeen
but I still hold a grasp
to the tingling touch of your
raspy brown hair

I'd like to feel your eyes
watch my movements
I want to think
that as I walk
your eyes trail my hips
as years get older
and hearts get colder
the sun still stands bolder
leaving enough room for
an angel to guide us home

I'll admit I mess up
more times than none
and my age doesn't improve things
at home or on the road
with bosses and workers
and jealous graduates
that I've found love
and no one can take that away

SOUL ENOUGH

Psychofairy — Faerie Whispers | poetry for the deep in heart

WHAT SHE KNOWS

She sits by the window
gazing forward at an
empty mailbox and a
crooked brown fence
waiting for her husband
to come home...

but what she doesn't know
is that a lady names
Carrie started work
with him today
wearing tiny little shirts
and long, tight skirts
with a waist that could
squeeze through a
white gold wedding band

but what she doesn't know
is that he's coming late
because he wanted to
buy his wife a little something
-
so he goes to a gas mart
and buys a few roses and
beer.

She sits by the window
with her chin on her
hands,
expecting the driveway
to cry, but this day
is different, because
her man knew how
to say no to a
woman who'd probably
never let him go

but when he drives up
and gets out of the car
he lifts his arms up
with an open, waiting hug
and she sees his life
behind his back

what this lady knows,
is that life doesn't
hide behind windows
and being married
means turning away
and remembering
your true love
at home...

154 Psychofairy | Faerie Whispers | poetry for the deep in heart

Driving

he sits at a red light
popping his chin
to the beat of the radio
waiting, waiting

standing on the wind
means dancing with the moon
and blowing down the breeze
means screaming
at the birds in the sky

he's ready to go
his foot on the pedal
but he holds himself back
stalling, stalling

dance with your heart
and then dance with the rain
don't let thoughts
leave you out on a trip
through nature's heyday

he's now pushing hard,
plowing the gas
knowing life has moved forward
and all storms lay stuck in the past

Psychofairy — Faerie Whispers | poetry for the deep in heart

Spilling OUT

there you are
selling out
enjoying her company
are you sure
she won't mind
is this place
really fine
grab her hand and ask

baby if love and hate
would meet tonight
would you stay with me
despite the fight
and let me start all over again -

here you are
spilling out
falling for his words
are you sure
he won't mind
you know this
place is too cold
to be alone -
grab his hand
and ask

156 Psychofairy — Faerie Whispers | poetry for the deep in heart

Silent fires

you've been chained to your spirit
for so long that
your soul has no room to breathe
your body aches
with carelessness
and your mind speaks out with fear
I don't know what
stands between us now
but a wall that won't fall down
a light could swallow our space
but our feet would steal our pride

don't let your heart
fall silent to any fires
that I start
don't let regret
change your beliefs
with me
even when you feel obliged

hold on to your broken wings
and let your feathers fall
wounds will heal
and hearts will seal
and dreams will
be remembered after all

I was dreaming about swimming swans
early Saturday morning
when he called.
Usually I start off kind of groggy
before my toothbrush fights
its way to a mumbling mouth
or before my toaster
feels the presence of pop-tarts
but that day I stood tall
like an adult sunflower
unaware if I was still sleeping
or maybe to acknowledge my message
on his answering machine,
or perhaps to find out
whether I liked him.
Either way,
I called him back hours later
then met at work again,
discussing the usual topics
couples do on their first night together.
But this is not a date
just a mere colliding of thoughts
we locked eyes
joking about past lovers,
cracking comments on turnoffs.
I had never hugged a cop before
until we embraced before he left
I felt his arms pulling me like vines
and I was his plant
still nurtured by the sun
and wild greenery

EMBRACE

158 Psychofairy Faerie Whispers | poetry for the deep in heart

He spoke to me the other day and I
looked into his frosty eyes
and I wished he would say something
that would make me smile
he said - girl you could be so
beautiful if you'd
work out a little and if you'd
wear some smaller clothes
but I said, man I want you to see me
just the way I am, which means
look into these tender eyes that say
I'm beautiful, I'm beautiful
so beautiful inside
I don't need no man to tell me otherwise
I am beautiful and I get
more beautiful by the size
he said, girl, I don't mean no harm
I just always speak my mind
please forgive me and not forget me, cause
people always tell me that I'm lucky
when they see you by my side...
you're beautiful, you're beautiful
so beautiful, my dear - how could I not
see it before, please don't close the door.

Beautiful by the size

Psychofairy
Faerie Whispers | poetry for the deep in heart

I can still smell your scent on this
blanket, your cologne now fills my blood
I can still feel your sweat beside me
on the pillow that still sits
the light will sing me to sleep tonight
and the air will tuck me in
I can't wait to see you once again
tomorrow will you call
or have you waited for this hour
you've got your piece but I haven't got mine, I still
wait for your calls, I still
sing your favorite songs, I will
not forget the sound of your voice
tomorrow will you call or has
last moment fulfilled you
is forever even on your mint, bet not
but if you ever want to talk, just
call me anytime
he knows I will stay awake tonight
and every time clocks chime
the hours drift away, he will
call in the morning, I'm sure he will
tell me how his dreams evolved, that he
smelled me while he slept.

DEAD RINGER

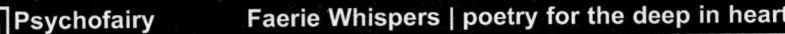

johnny

Looking at Johnny was worse
than peering into the eyes of desperation
I didn't know the twenty bucks
I asked dad to lend him
would become his suicide needle
sometimes I listen for his fists
echoing off doors like he did
that night at the eve of twilight -
pounding and beating with impatience
maybe he still paces the patio
with his fingers leaving wide trails
through his charcoal-stained hair...
his silent attempts for help,
his lasts regretful breaths -
and ungraceful ending for a father of three
where all that remained was an unfinished
apology to his wife,
vowing to visit once he was clean,
he resembled a well
deeply grounded, cold and empty.
I miss days at church
when he'd take up offerings
or sing Spanish songs to the congregation
maybe we were last to know of his drag habits
maybe we were to engrossed with ourselves
to care.

my own grace, unreflected

I glanced at myself, practiced
smiling, turning sideways, tucked in my belly
sprayed hair for extra hold, retouched the bobby pins,
plucked sporadic eyebrow hairs that got away,
perfumed the neck, lotioned the arms,
readjusted the girdle, made sure the pantyhose
were control top, leaned over scooped my breasts
checked my fingernails, toenails -- a perfect match
my make up flawless as porcelain,
posture as graceful as an Oscar,
arms, legs, pits now waxed and bared
shoes lent me three more inches --
I had never felt so pretty, so beautiful, so immaculate
and I called my husband into the room
straightened the long evening gown once more,
smoothed away soft wrinkles and stood there
with my whitened teeth shining, waiting for him to
sweep me off my feet with adoring compliments...
I ask "How do I look?" - he must not have noticed
he looks, pauses, responds with "Good."

Psychofairy   Faerie Whispers | poetry for the deep in heart

oriental music with soft mandolins and harps
ripening the air at the Chinese diner
so calm and tender
almost hypnotic
servers tiptoe with quiet feet on flat heels
hair up, fingernails trimmed
so hushed and reserved from the crowd

kitchen doors swing open and
gentle sounds of breathing strings
turn into a love ballad by Leann Rimes --
doors shut once more
enchanting harps return...

I couldn't help but raise an eyebrow
every time a server would retreat
I would catch another earful
of country-pop while
Chinese cooks led separate lives

Secret China

MY MORNINGS

the first alarm goes off

I ignore it

my husband grabs me from behind

cradles me

our dog runs the marathon on our legs

we shoo her

she comes back

the radio alarm turns on

the dj is telling a bad joke

I doze back to sleep

my husband tells me to wake up

I ignore him

he buries his face in my back

holds me tighter, wraps me in a blanket

get up, he says again

I barely open one eye to see the time

in two more minutes, I'll be late

but that's two more minutes I can sleep

the third alarm goes off

I ignore that too

my husband is lying behind me

get up, he mumbles

I ignore him

I open an eye to peek at the time again

I'm five minutes late

I hop out of bed as if on fire

and yell at husband for making me late

164 Psychofairy

Faerie Whispers | poetry for the deep in heart

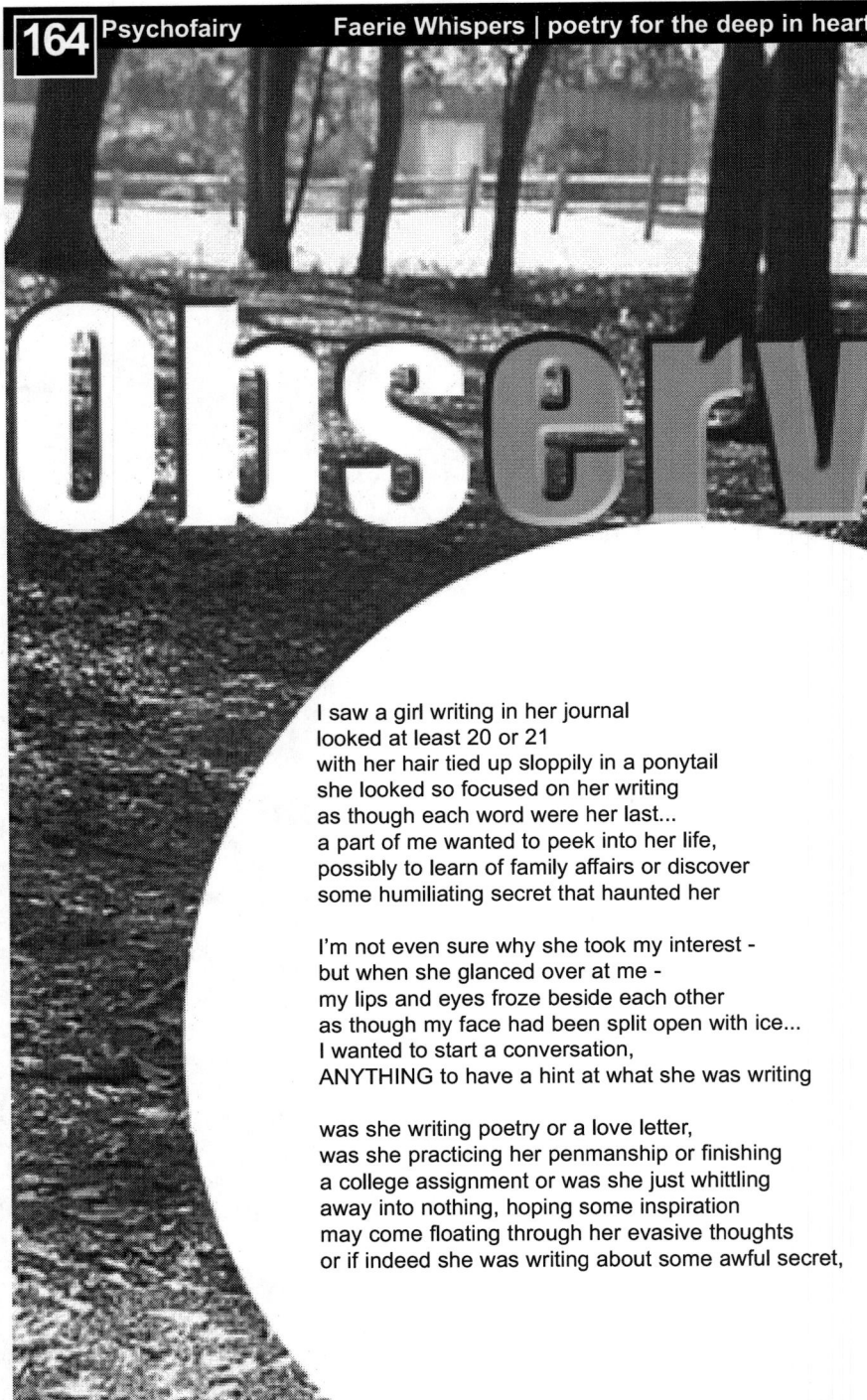

Observ

I saw a girl writing in her journal
looked at least 20 or 21
with her hair tied up sloppily in a ponytail
she looked so focused on her writing
as though each word were her last...
a part of me wanted to peek into her life,
possibly to learn of family affairs or discover
some humiliating secret that haunted her

I'm not even sure why she took my interest -
but when she glanced over at me -
my lips and eyes froze beside each other
as though my face had been split open with ice...
I wanted to start a conversation,
ANYTHING to have a hint at what she was writing

was she writing poetry or a love letter,
was she practicing her penmanship or finishing
a college assignment or was she just whittling
away into nothing, hoping some inspiration
may come floating through her evasive thoughts
or if indeed she was writing about some awful secret,

Psychofairy **Faerie Whispers | poetry for the deep in heart**

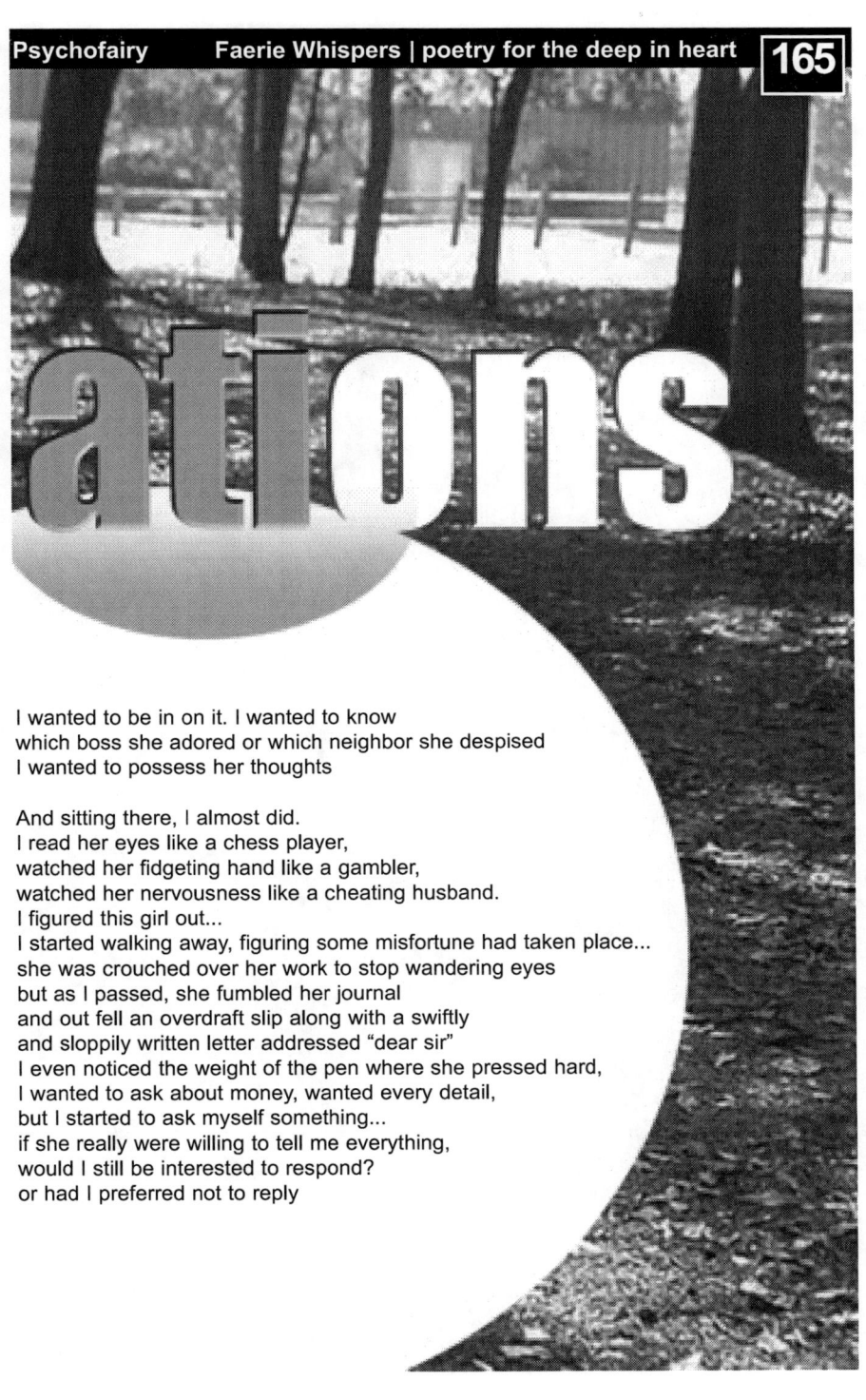

I wanted to be in on it. I wanted to know
which boss she adored or which neighbor she despised
I wanted to possess her thoughts

And sitting there, I almost did.
I read her eyes like a chess player,
watched her fidgeting hand like a gambler,
watched her nervousness like a cheating husband.
I figured this girl out...
I started walking away, figuring some misfortune had taken place...
she was crouched over her work to stop wandering eyes
but as I passed, she fumbled her journal
and out fell an overdraft slip along with a swiftly
and sloppily written letter addressed "dear sir"
I even noticed the weight of the pen where she pressed hard,
I wanted to ask about money, wanted every detail,
but I started to ask myself something...
if she really were willing to tell me everything,
would I still be interested to respond?
or had I preferred not to reply

Psychofairy   Faerie Whispers | poetry for the deep in heart

as Beautiful

you are as beautiful
as Boston at 8 am
when the light from
the sun shines on
the miles of cars
sitting on the highway

you are as precious
as San Francisco
at our favorite park
where the dew
is so strong
it could fill our cups

you are as lovely
as Niagara Falls
in the middle of
a cold winter
where all the ice
freezes your breath
so I can hold it

Exotic Eyes

The leaves in the girl's hair
tucked behind her ear
remind me of tangles
that make the head bleed
when pulled too hard -
from the left
she looks flawless
from the right
she looks like me
her eyes restless
tired, stressed
but alive...
darkness under her eyes
make her exotic
and it draws me
that with leaves,
branches in hair
entangled by wind
she still holds beauty.

nothing else

Romance as beautiful as black and pink roses
sheets browner than most Dutch of chocolates
lips redder than the hottest blush
I crave the bed we sleep in
the way you spoon with me
the way you hold my back to your stomach
and how your hands feel so warm
no matter how cold the room
I've known love before
but never as real as this
never had I looked into eyes like yours
and melted in them
never had someone touched me
in a way where I felt completely taken
where I felt nothing else in the world
hair as fine as the silkiest fabric
hands as smooth as the smile on your face
music as gentle as the pillow we share
tonight we fall in love again

Psychofairy   Faerie Whispers | poetry for the deep in heart   **169**

for Michelle

She looked as though
this day had waited for her
as if these months
had given her this glow
standing there
behind church doors
waiting for the march
I held her hand
preparing to glide the runner
she stops, turns
fingers her mouth
as if gagging
but she was simply
removing a tongue ring
which she thought
would damper the day --
there she, in white elegance,
hair up, nails polished,
body waxed, shined, perfumed
and right before she
walks down,
struggles to remove a
metal piercing form her mouth...
I stared at her imperfection
catching a glimpse of
what photos never capture.

The Bridal RING

| 170 | Psychofairy | Faerie Whispers | poetry for the deep in heart |

how small

I will never forget that terrible stench
coming out of his mouth
smell of eggs, fish and mustard
and he would lick my face, neck, body
and no matter how much I inched backwards
he would move with me
the look in those eyes reminded me
of how small I had become
beneath such large, strong arms
ripping me like frayed cotton

Psychofairy
Faerie Whispers | poetry for the deep in heart

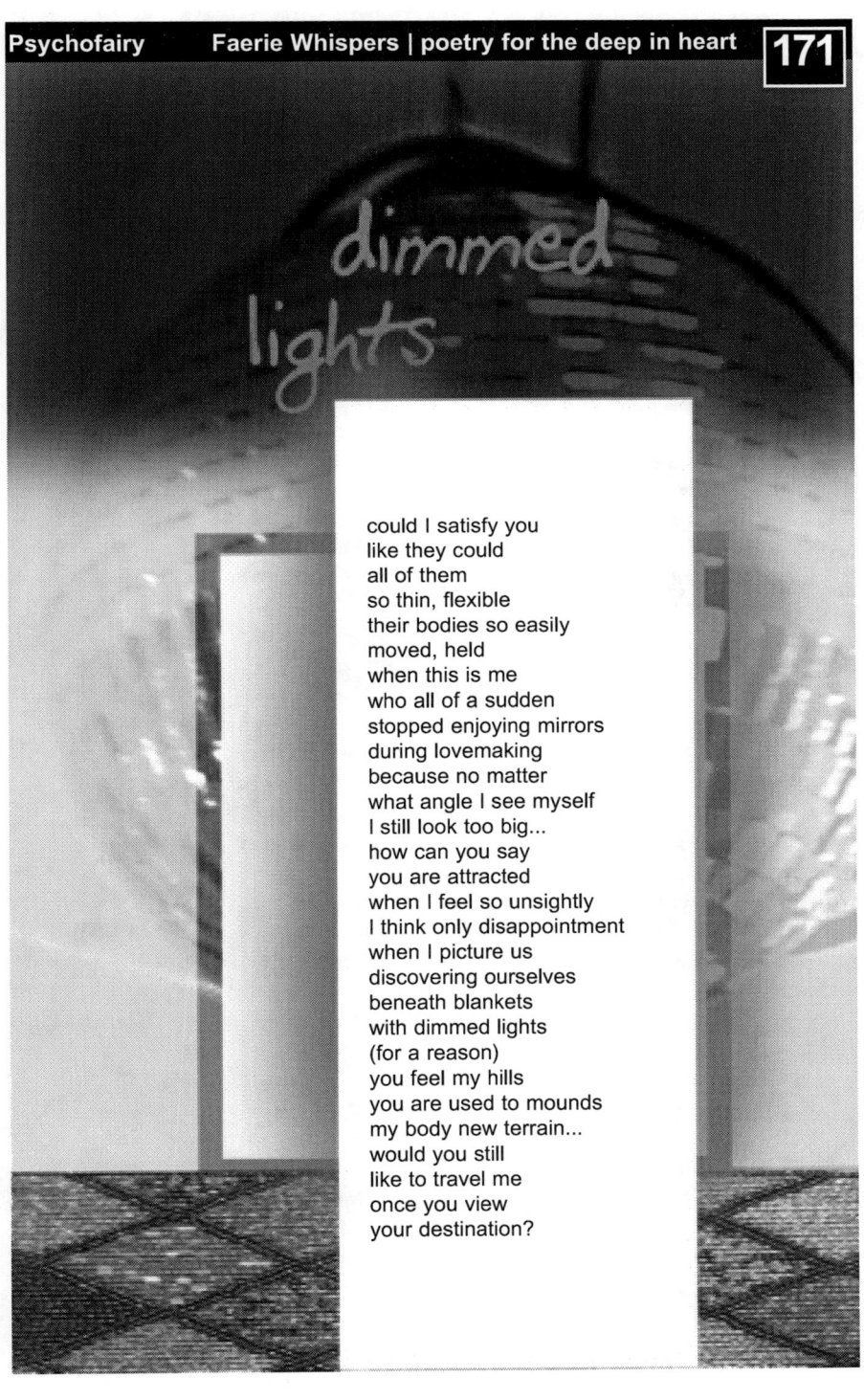

dimmed lights

could I satisfy you
like they could
all of them
so thin, flexible
their bodies so easily
moved, held
when this is me
who all of a sudden
stopped enjoying mirrors
during lovemaking
because no matter
what angle I see myself
I still look too big...
how can you say
you are attracted
when I feel so unsightly
I think only disappointment
when I picture us
discovering ourselves
beneath blankets
with dimmed lights
(for a reason)
you feel my hills
you are used to mounds
my body new terrain...
would you still
like to travel me
once you view
your destination?

Letter to

the thought of you warms me, and even on the coldest day
I think of you, so lonely, so beautiful, so wanting
and I get chills on my arms, and immediately start writing
I have tears of love and joy for you and then I warm up
right now as I write this I was freezing and just THINKING about you -
I get this warm sensation all over my body, my feet were ice cold
and now they feel like they have touched the most amazing fire
you absolutely amaze me as a person, as a man, as a lover,
as a mentor, as a soulmate, there is no way I can describe what you mean to me
and it is agonizing that I must be here, but it only makes it better
knowing love like this cannot be denied or mistaken, even though confusing
and at times doubtful - but feelings very real and it feels better
knowing that time heals all wounds and one day there will be no more wounds
and the two of us will heal together with no scars
no more hurt, no more pain, no more agony, we will find solace
in companionship, and I find that now, even so far apart
you make breathing worthwhile, you make waking up a joy
you make going to work tolerable, because I know I can spend every spare moment
daydreaming about our time together, you make sleeping wonderful
cause I have the most restful sleep, I think only peaceful, sweet thoughts
I think only the good of you, every wonderful thing about you
and then I just see this amazing man and you sweep me off my feet
and I dream and dream and wake up feeling refreshed
as though part of me has been fulfilled so incredibly happy
I am so happy to have you, so happy to know you, so happy to have even MET you
meeting was a coincidence, but not really...we were meant to be, I think
that's what makes me warm because I love thinking about you
it makes me smile, makes me laugh, makes me blush, makes me feel so beautiful
and no one makes me feel beautiful anymore
and I feel like I am coming out of my shell again
which is a feeling no one has given me in a long time
I feel accepted, do you know how hard that is?
I feel loved, I feel amazing...the moment I step on a computer
the first thing I do is check to see if you are on or what you have written
I crave the scent of your words in everything you say
I cannot go a minute online without thinking of you - it is awful
you have put this spell on me and it is eating me

Psychofairy   Faerie Whispers | poetry for the deep in heart

my Love

I am captured for life and you are this amazing man almost out of reach
you are almost like a brilliant poster on a wall that people look up to
and now that I can have you I want you even more
and at times I almost shake thinking of you, you make my arms twitch sometimes
I wish I were there to tell you all the thoughts in my mind you are so amazing
I have so much I want to say so much I want to do, so much!
I just feel bare without you and I need you to clothe me with
your hands, your eyes, your feelings
I would love you to clothe my bare heart with your hands
that makes me feel so warm, so WARM
I wish you could feel this ... I feel so so so ... ugh! there are no words!
you are a guitar and I want to be your strings
I want to read you poetry every day of your life
I want to be the one to make YOU dinner, massage YOUR feet, buy YOU gifts
I want to spend time with YOU, give YOU pleasure, treat YOU good
make YOU feel beautiful, let YOU feel love, let YOU see everything good in life
you do too much for other people
I want to be the one to do something for you, I want to melt your heart
I want to be the one to melt it, I want to be the one person who didn't do you wrong
the one person who was good to you and never left, never cheated, never hurt you
never neglected you, never abandoned you, never ignored you
never took you for granted, never unappreciated you
I want to be the woman that makes you smile, just smile
that's all I want from you ... a nice smile
to let me know you are happy and when you DON'T smile, I will try my best to
MAKE you smile ... I hate to see you sad, I will always make you happy
even when I go psycho, I will always be there to make you happy
you are so beautiful, I look at your picture at work
and think of an angel ... I have pictures of you on my filing cabinet
that no one sees but me and I stare and stare and stare
and catch myself giddily happy for no reason
I will start giggling and smiling just looking at you
you tickle me with your smile, your charm and your tuffy
I love you both and I love you hon ... I wish I could say so much more
you should see the poems I write about you - I have so much in my head right now
but my feelings for you are real - I may be confused about a lot of things
but not about my love for you .... please remember that

174 Psychofairy — Faerie Whispers | poetry for the deep in heart

JULY

He held her for the first time
after the fact, smelling her
in a newfound ownership
as if he now possessed her.

Psychofairy — Faerie Whispers | poetry for the deep in heart

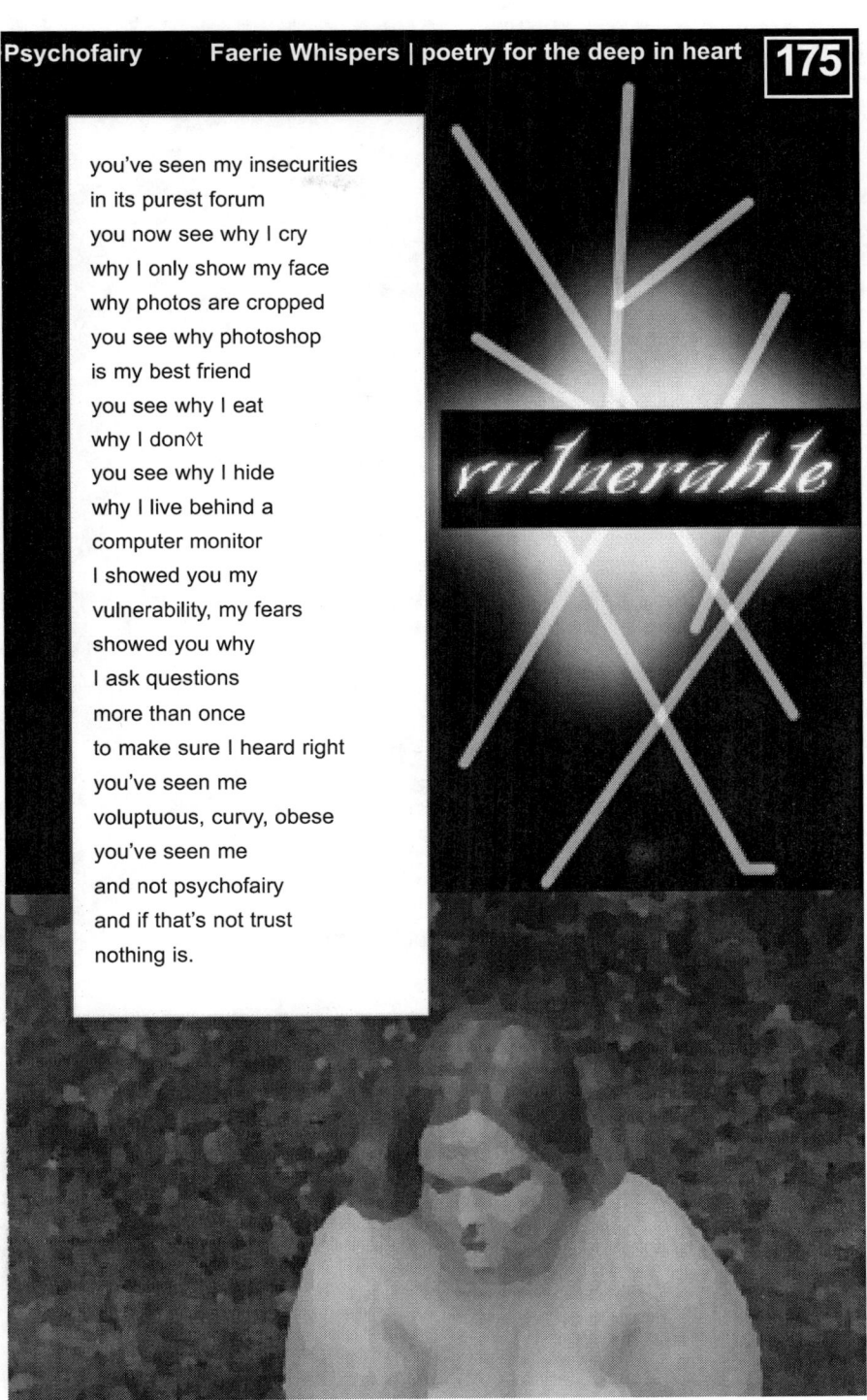

you've seen my insecurities
in its purest forum
you now see why I cry
why I only show my face
why photos are cropped
you see why photoshop
is my best friend
you see why I eat
why I don◊t
you see why I hide
why I live behind a
computer monitor
I showed you my
vulnerability, my fears
showed you why
I ask questions
more than once
to make sure I heard right
you've seen me
voluptuous, curvy, obese
you've seen me
and not psychofairy
and if that's not trust
nothing is.

176 | Psychofairy — Faerie Whispers | poetry for the deep in heart

Not hearing your voice
is more disappointing than a bad haircut,
may as well cut my heart out
with silver scissors.
My emotions have been trimmed
by other stylists,
zigzagging in every way.

trimming emotions

Psychofairy | Faerie Whispers | poetry for the deep in heart

no need for names

he masturbates
like, all the time
even after dinner
and he watches too much porn
he turns the channel
the minute I walk in the room
pretend there is no video in the vcr...
he looks up at me
wondering if I notice
and of course, I always do

sex isn't all that great
never has been
never feels very good
always over before it starts
I want to imagine him as someone else
the world must think we are perfect

one day I will walk away from this
meet someone fully clothed
who has sex longer than 10 minutes
meet someone who watches
videos of little ol' me instead
of Jasmine St. Clair

178 | Psychofairy | Faerie Whispers | poetry for the deep in heart

yes, I know
I am torturing myself
it's my fault
I wanted you
you were pushed,
edged seduced
you were handled
with delicate hands
vulnerable hands
I let myself go
then stopped
begged for mercy
cried, guilty of love
I want more
I hold myself hostage
needing freedom
but also security
why can't I have both
why must I choose?

Psychofairy
Faerie Whispers | poetry for the deep in heart

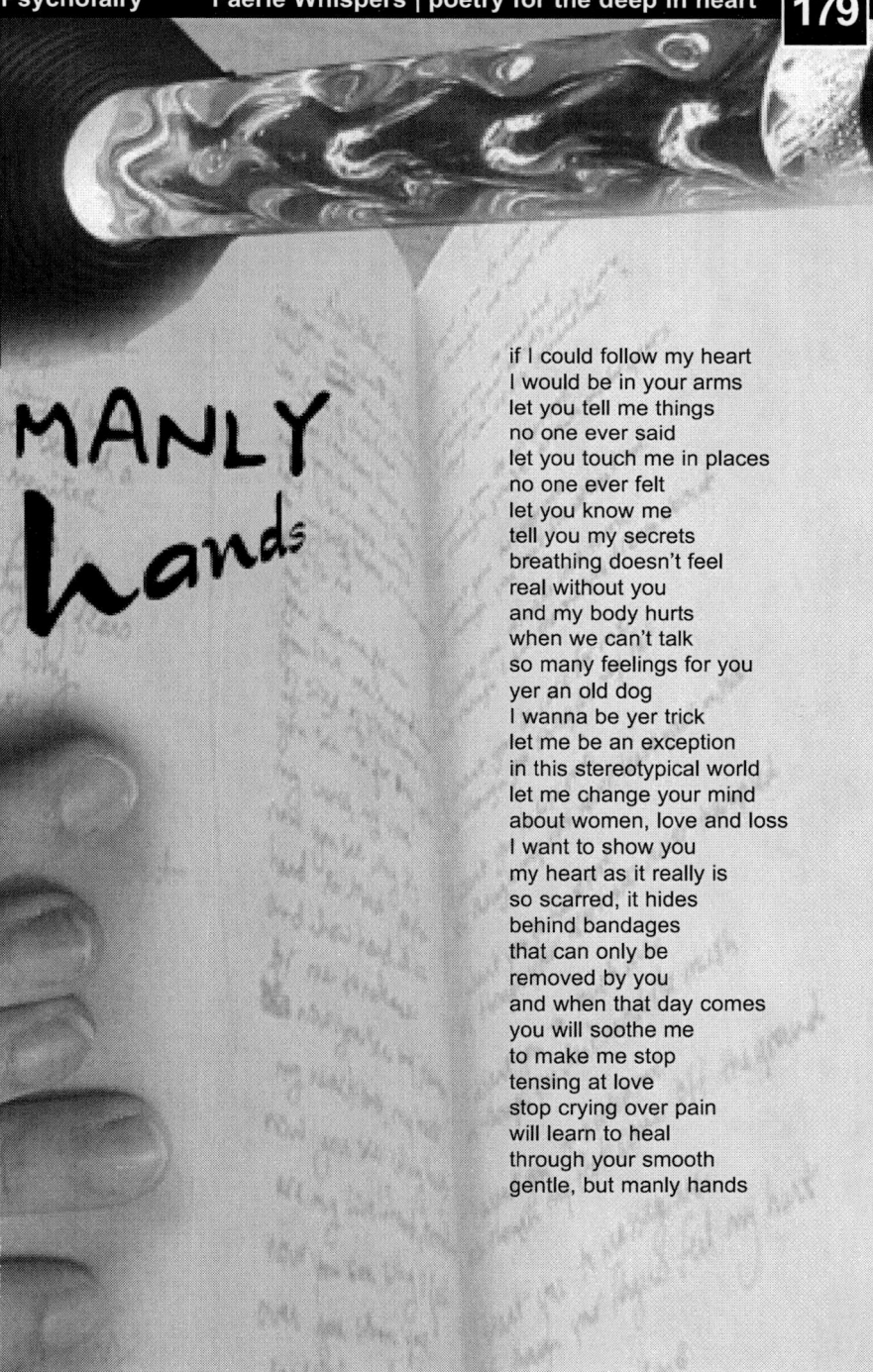

MANLY hands

if I could follow my heart
I would be in your arms
let you tell me things
no one ever said
let you touch me in places
no one ever felt
let you know me
tell you my secrets
breathing doesn't feel
real without you
and my body hurts
when we can't talk
so many feelings for you
yer an old dog
I wanna be yer trick
let me be an exception
in this stereotypical world
let me change your mind
about women, love and loss
I want to show you
my heart as it really is
so scarred, it hides
behind bandages
that can only be
removed by you
and when that day comes
you will soothe me
to make me stop
tensing at love
stop crying over pain
will learn to heal
through your smooth
gentle, but manly hands

180 | Psychofairy — Faerie Whispers | poetry for the deep in heart

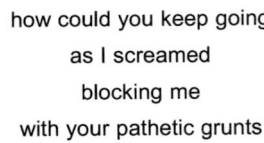

how could you keep going
as I screamed
blocking me
with your pathetic grunts

how could you not look down
see me crying
as you hurt me
tearing me

how do you zip yourself
as if I was a to-do list
your chore

how the hell
do you get
off

Psychofairy — Faerie Whispers | poetry for the deep in heart

Now you see

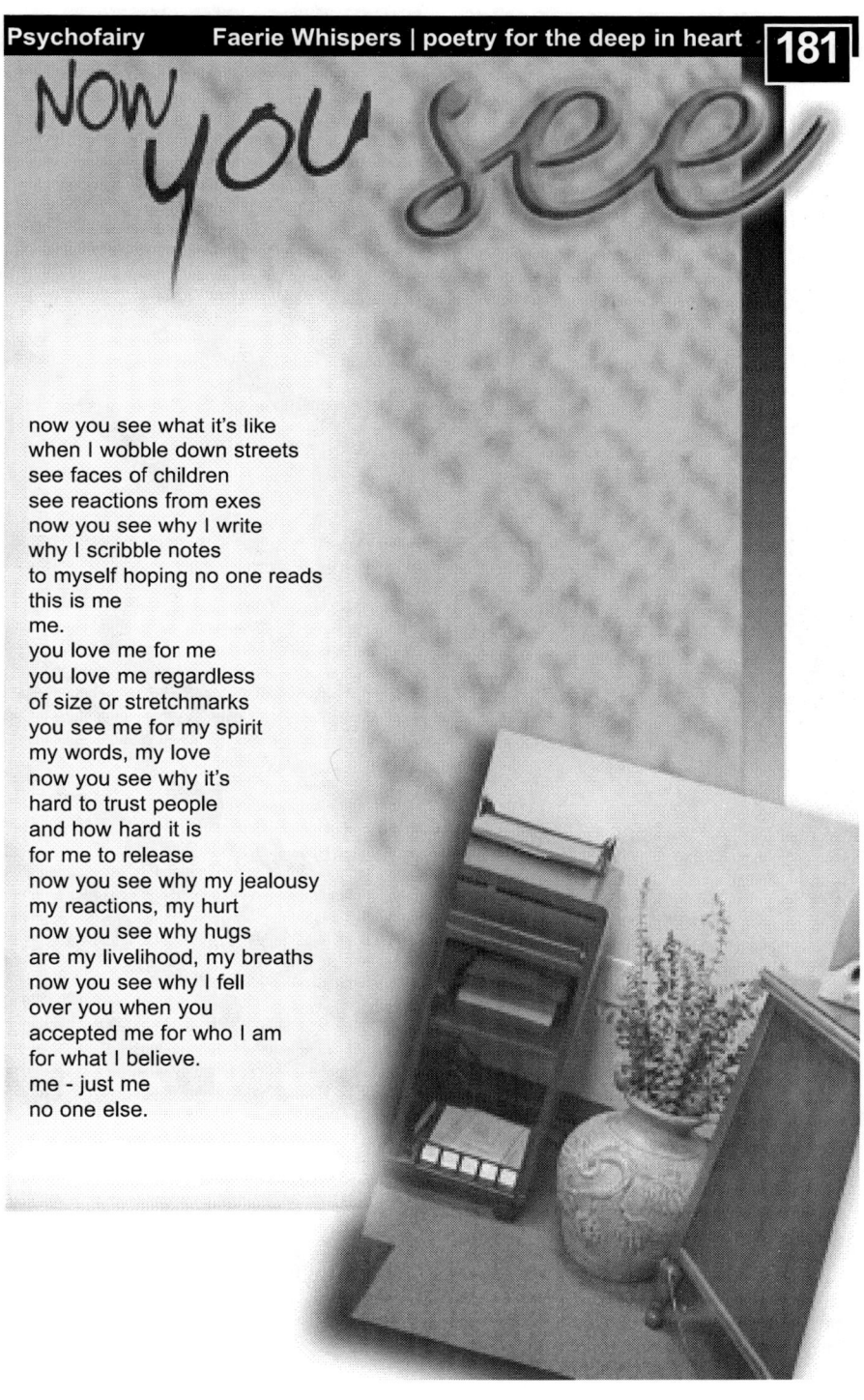

now you see what it's like
when I wobble down streets
see faces of children
see reactions from exes
now you see why I write
why I scribble notes
to myself hoping no one reads
this is me
me.
you love me for me
you love me regardless
of size or stretchmarks
you see me for my spirit
my words, my love
now you see why it's
hard to trust people
and how hard it is
for me to release
now you see why my jealousy
my reactions, my hurt
now you see why hugs
are my livelihood, my breaths
now you see why I fell
over you when you
accepted me for who I am
for what I believe.
me - just me
no one else.

1995

All four of us sat on the sofa

me the only girl

they, with raging hormones

wanted to feel me

feel a woman

get a quick arousal

and at first I thought it was funny

and let them

cause they were my friends

and I trusted

I always trusted

wrong people

I believed I wouldn't get hurt

and soon innocent laughter

turned to screams

and sounds of ripping panties

I have never learned to love
every man has always left
even my brother did
lifeless but alive
he never taught me how to drive
never taught me how to love
he never got to play basketball
just sits in a wheelchair year after year

I always loved male friends
I'd secretly want them to be him
be the big brother I never had
I would latch on to them, but never love
too afraid to hurt again
"How come you had to drown?
why couldn't you have just sat down?
WHY was I not old enough to stop you?
why won't you ANSWER me when I talk?
I know you hear me."

it's hard to be between so many divorces
watch fathers leave
get attached only to have them stripped
I needed to learn love,
no one would teach me
one could have stayed

when I found a man who wanted me,
I said I love you for the first time
we get engaged, he cheated
how could I love that?
left him for good, left my family, left all
no man ever stayed except God
no woman ever loved except my sister
no one ever told me they loved me and meant it
no one let me love in return

now I am married
my husband is perfect, they say
treats me like royalty
but I still don't know love
I want this to last but
nothing ever does
and they always promise to stay
but I have lost my heart
I feel nothing
his "I love you's" are just words

Psychofairy

Faerie Whispers | poetry for the deep in heart

words from a child

I can tell the sound of her car
in the driveway...
the sound of those eleven keys
unlocking the front door
I fear the turn of the brass door knob,
footsteps on mauve carpet...

I can always tell her mood
by the sound her purse makes
I wish this blanket could make me invisible
so many nights wishing to be loved
I secretly pray to be someone else
to live another life
or to just...live

I scribble in hidden journals
too scared she might read them
too scared she might burn them
flipping through pages
is a brutal reminder

OLDER MAN

I would have married you
if you were twenty years younger
or if these vows didn't matter

I kick myself for thinking of things
that tempt me
and sometimes it hurts
can't simply run away

I feel almost ashamed
that my heart, again
belongs to an older man
so much wiser and mature than me
someone who would cradle me
let me feel like a child
and make up for the love
I missed growing up

my husband sits a room away
begging for attention
he always needs attention
I am smothered with love from him
any other woman would
die for a love like that

I want what I can't have
do things to my husband
I want to do to you
and while he leans back with eyes closed
you are the image I see

this skin is just flesh

these pounds are just food

my hands may be bigger

my back may feel softer

but I am still me

I can love myself

without you

Psychofairy
Faerie Whispers | poetry for the deep in heart

I want you to cherish me
as though we have never loved

I want you to hold me
as though your hands don't care
if they can reach around me

I want you to accept me
as though you've known me for years

I want you to keep me
as though you can't live without me

I want you to make love to me
as though I am the one you dream of

I want you to care for me
as though you shrug at my fat

I want you to kiss me
as though my lips never leave your mind

I want you to have me
as though your heart was never trampled

I want you to touch me
as though you don't mind the mush

I want you to sweep me
as though my feet come off the ground

I want you to massage me
as though your fingers feel my hurt

I want you to taste me
as though my skin is sweet

I want you to take me
as though all the photos in the world
and all the looks didn't matter
and it's just the two of us
sitting beside each other
with melted hearts
knowing nothing but trust.

Psychofairy   Faerie Whispers | poetry for the deep in heart

why does it hurt to breathe
when you aren't around
think of things I want to do
write what I never say
living without you
is worse than Chinese torture
so many obstacles
so many hearts
I should feel blessed
we can still talk
but hiding feelings is so fake
so difficult
so hard
like hurtful knots
squeezing and twisting within me
how can I feel love
so strong like this
when I know we
can never be.

Psychofairy — Faerie Whispers | poetry for the deep in heart

WONDERING

Every time we talk
we get closer
I picture you sitting there
looking at my pictures
I wonder what you think
when you look at me
wonder if I'm still beautiful
wondering if one bad picture
turns you away forever
you love my like water
you love to hold me
cleanse me
I am a drain without you
being sucked out
my life force stricken
with marital confusion
all this is so hard
decisions mean so much
what if I choose wrong
what if our closeness fades
what if I lost both of you
only fears eat me alive
my dreams waken me
I feel so torn --

Psychofairy   Faerie Whispers | poetry for the deep in heart

I Choose You

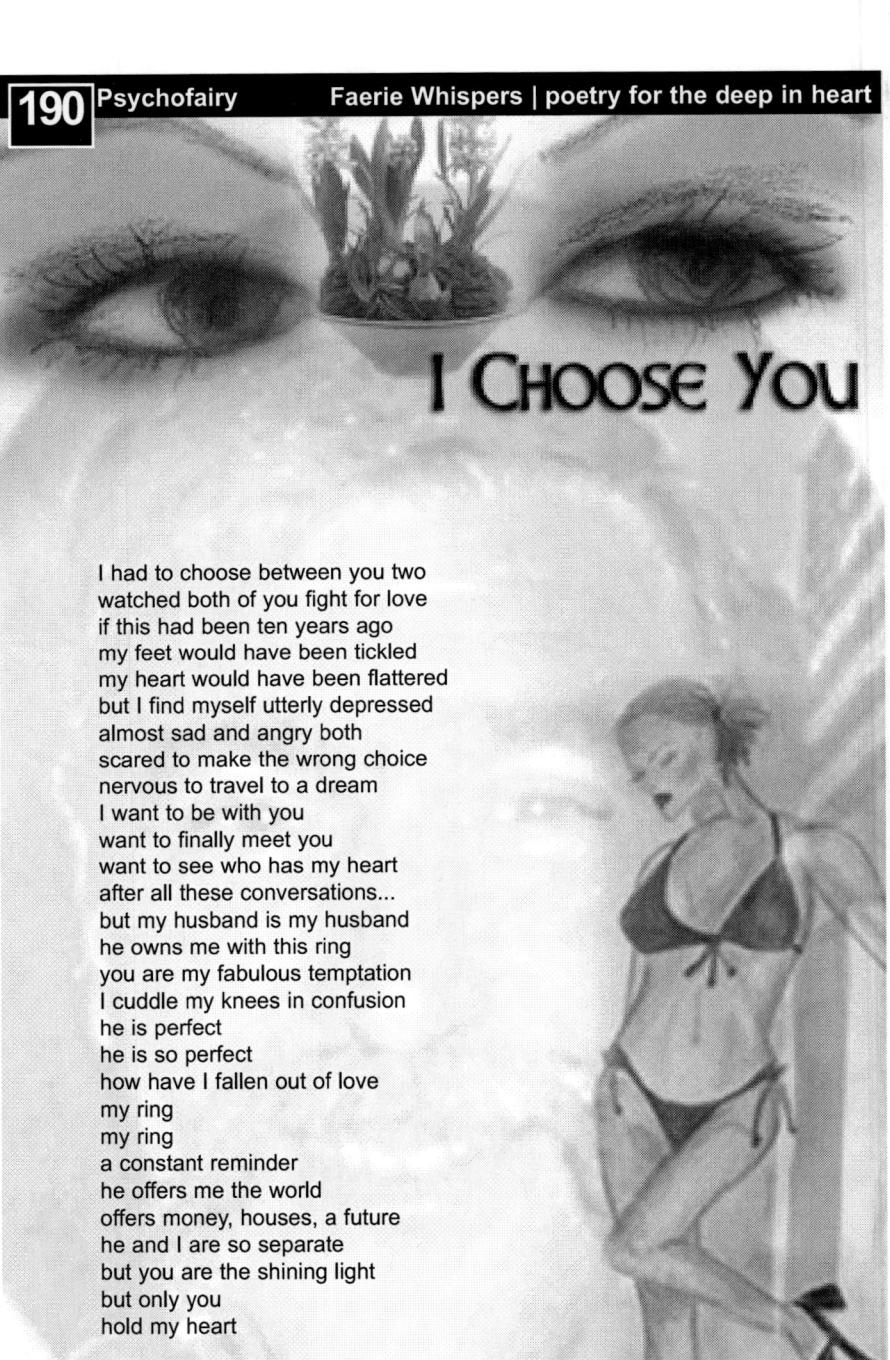

I had to choose between you two
watched both of you fight for love
if this had been ten years ago
my feet would have been tickled
my heart would have been flattered
but I find myself utterly depressed
almost sad and angry both
scared to make the wrong choice
nervous to travel to a dream
I want to be with you
want to finally meet you
want to see who has my heart
after all these conversations...
but my husband is my husband
he owns me with this ring
you are my fabulous temptation
I cuddle my knees in confusion
he is perfect
he is so perfect
how have I fallen out of love
my ring
my ring
a constant reminder
he offers me the world
offers money, houses, a future
he and I are so separate
but you are the shining light
but only you
hold my heart

Psychofairy

Faerie Whispers | poetry for the deep in heart

I think the worst
part is that I can◊t talk about it

no one knows
not even my family

and I still feel pain
every December 5th

and feel stared
as if being undressed

constantly being eyed
by strangers

if only I had been a boy
I wouldn't have been so frail

so easily broken
so painfully taken

EASILY BROKEN

Psychofairy — Faerie Whispers | poetry for the deep in heart

love & murder

love, Undenied

honey I love you so much
I want to shout it to the world
I don't care if it is wrong
don't care of society shuns me
God will not
you are the reason I wake
you are why I sleep, breathe
I feel you warm on my skin
from hundreds of miles away
and your presence is overwhelming
our love cannot be denied
no more shame, guilt
you are not hidden, my love
I want to show the world
who I love
let them see what I gave up
I have never known love
to be this strong
so strong I could rip these pages
I just want to hold you
feel you, feel loved in return
why don't people understand
what I have without you
is a show, no love
only you give me this
if only the world could
read my thoughts
this would makes so much sense
I ache without you
I cry without you
I toss in bed with someone else
with no desires at all
except to be with you
I have been faithful
so faithful
I will leave, honey
only want to be with you.

Psychofairy | Faerie Whispers | poetry for the deep in heart

when I show you everything
I will have no reason to doubt
you will understand my nervousness
feel what troubles me
see why I cry
more reason to hold me
will you still tell me I am beautiful,
remind me of who I am?
I want more than this
want you to know me
opening up is so hard
you've only seen the good
when you've seen everything
I will trust

TRUSTING WHO I DO NOT SEE

Psychofairy

Faerie Whispers | poetry for the deep in heart

SHADOW

I envy my shadow

always tall and thin

with exaggerated features

in all the right places

as it follows the sun

gracefully beside me.

I watch my silhouette

and secretly wish it were me...

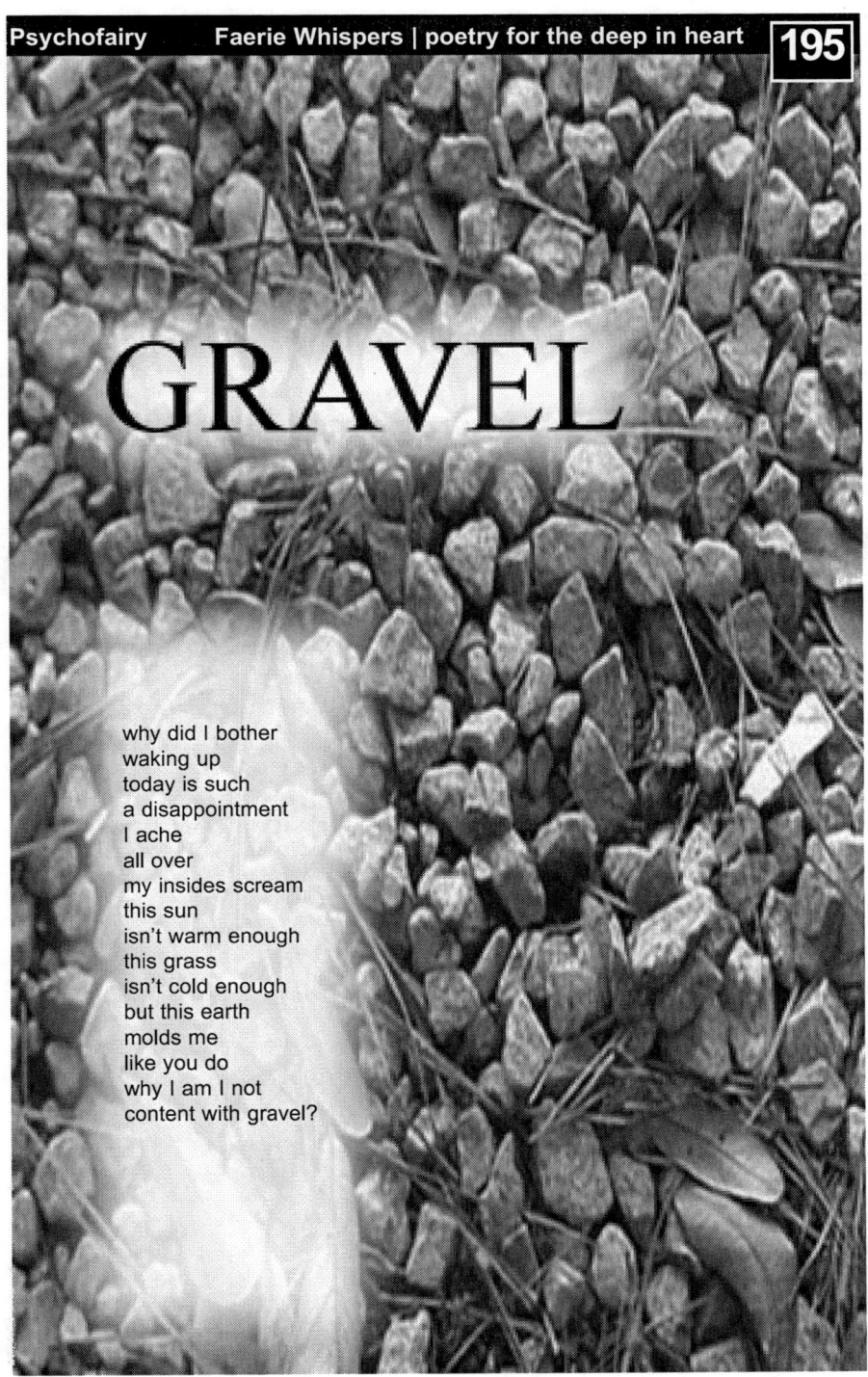

GRAVEL

why did I bother
waking up
today is such
a disappointment
I ache
all over
my insides scream
this sun
isn't warm enough
this grass
isn't cold enough
but this earth
molds me
like you do
why I am I not
content with gravel?

Psychofairy — Faerie Whispers | poetry for the deep in heart

it's funny

it's funny how you worry about your age
the way I do my weight
but neither of us mind the other
it's funny how I love you
even more than my husband
and how people are so quick
to judge, throw rocks at us
without knowing my story
they think marriage should be forever
so how could I love you...
but people do not know my home...
don't know the sex addictions
of the person I live with
or the night he forced himself in me
left me screaming, bleeding, crying
then claimed not to remember a thing
it's funny how people don't wanna hear it
and would rather me stick around
to let it happen again
because the Bible says so...
it's funny how I am giving up everything
my house, my job, so much money
all for something called love
taking a leap of faith, trust
to a man so many miles away
that cradles my heart like a child
and tells me I am beautiful
even when my thighs disagree -
it's funny how I can look at you
and feel so utterly in love
so incredibly content, peaceful, safe
but have to dodge stones
from onlookers who only see
things in black and white

At The Water's Edge

at the water's edge
I have become myself
this cold wind on my back
feels like God pushing me
God kissing me all over
even my toes through these sandals
what a humbling moment
for me and this lake
talk to each other
just the two of us
ignoring this cold
endless turning of journal papers
if I fell, God would rescue me
if I stumble, He would pull me out
my fears, at this very moment
just sitting on top of these
mounds of sharp, course rocks
have left, there are no more doubts
if I cried, these tan stones would
turn gray, my emotions soak even sand
Lord take these feelings
throw them in the sea
I don't want my heart to skip like
a tossed pebble
dunk my in Your love
free me from my own mind
show me what I do not see
teach me what I have not learned
mold me into your servant

Psychofairy — Faerie Whispers | poetry for the deep in heart

ACKNOWLEDGEMENTS:

Too many people to list, that's for sure!!! But I would like to start off by thanking God because it's a miracle I'm alive especially since that whole 18-wheeler experience happened and I could have been buried! Not to mention countless experiences where miracles happened and it is a complete miracle to be alive! I would also like to thank my parents, especially my dad who first introduced me to poetry and always thrived in my talent and was never afraid to give (too many) compliments... so dad, thanks! Mom - even though you think some of my writing is outlandish, thanks for my first diary on my 10th birthday... which is what inspired me to write in the first place. I would like to thank my sister, Tammy - who even took off and got married without telling me - I forgive you and love you profusely! Dew tick! I gotta thank my brother, Abe, to whom most of my faith remains... one day you will be able to walk, talk and eat and you are one of the main reasons I choose to believe in miracles. Bum bum! I love you!

I would like to thank Willie James King, a poet who sorta kicked me into Creative Writing class and pushed me into auditioning into a fantastic school (and got in!) and believed in me when I didn't even believe in myself... gotta thank Jerry Lawrence and Nancy Scheetz, two of my Creative Writing teachers who REALLY showed me how to write from the heart - and gave me positive criticism which is something very rare people do. If it wasn't for you guys, most of my stuff would be so cliche.... thanks for showing me how to release the real me!

And in this stage of my life, I have a very addictive love for the forums at Secret Artists..and I must say some of the best friends in the world are in there... in fact, several people there gave me the extra push to putting out this book and I must thank them... I'm kinda afraid to mention everyone, because I'm so afraid to leave someone out... so I would like to thank you all as a whole! But a special shoutout to BouquetCatcher and BlueSage for suggesting I write this book....

I would like to thank some dear friends of mine: Chief aka Chris Crane, Lynne Vickers, Leah Heaton, Penny, Melissa, Ryan, Don, Mike, David, Michelle Collier, Jennifer Swindall, Karen, Tammy Harris, Shannon, Chris, Devin, Dylan, John Ford, Linda Abel, Myra Lewiski, Jessi Goodwin, Rhonda Ward, Jason Baisden, all my ex-crushes, flings, ex-boyfriends (many poems stem from you crazy people)...

I gotta especially thank David Grant and all Michael's D&D buddies for helping me pick out the name "Psychofairy" to be my official nickname.... it was a fantastic choice and catchy too!

I gotta thank my ex-fiance, for cheating on me so that I would open my eyes and marry someone else.... thanks for doing the world a favor! I would like to thank my husband, Michael for always being there and doing the smallest of things like turning on the light when I am awake at odd hours of the night typing on the computer and for bringing me drinks without me asking and for cooking for me when I am too wrapped up in writing to get up and do it myself.

I want to thank my online family -- my best friends in the world whom I have never even met, but yet we know so much about each other -- that includes Chief, Leya, Carola, and Amanda. I would like to mention the rest of the family life gang, but so many are joining us, that I don't wanna leave someone out - but I love you all so much!

oOoooOoooOoooh and I gotta thank YOU for picking up this book... it's people like you that give dreamers like me a dream come true... by buying this book, you have, in essence - made my wish a reality and for that, I am deeply indebted. Thank you!